# Thomas Reid's
# LECTURES ON NATURAL THEOLOGY (1780)

Transcribed from Student Notes, Edited and
with an Introduction
by
**Elmer H. Duncan**
Baylor University

with a new essay
"Reid: First Principles and Reason in the Lectures on Natural
Theology"
by
**William R. Eakin**

Copyright © 1981 by

**University Press of America, Inc.**

P.O. Box 19101, Washington, D.C. 20036

Printed in the United States of America

ISBN: 0-8191-1354-9 (Case)
0-8191-1355-7 (Perfect)

/

Library of Congress Catalog Card Number: 80-5964

FOR ROSEMARY

## ACKNOWLEDGMENTS

I am grateful to the Mitchell Library in Glasgow for permission to publish part of the lectures of Thomas Reid. I am also grateful to Baylor University and especially to William F. Cooper, now Dean of Faculty Development, and William G. Toland, Dean of the College of Arts and Sciences, for an eight-month sabbatical for the Summer and Fall of 1977 to work on transcribing and editing Thomas Reid's lectures on natural theology. I did not expect to take three years. In almost three years, nobody has even asked for a progress report--I think that says something (something good) about Baylor University. The text has a few Greek and Latin passages. I sought the expert assistance of Professor of Classics Richard C. Cutter; for some of the passages he conferred with his Chairman, Professor Roy F. Butler--I am grateful to both. I am also grateful for the constant support of my Chairman, William J. Kilgore, and my colleague Robert M. Baird.

Thanks are also due to a fine graduate student, William R. Eakin, who wrote one of the first papers (and, I think, a very interesting and thought provoking work) on Reid's natural theology.

Finally, manuscript preparation is all-important, and I cannot say enough about the work of the world's finest secretary, and my Chairman's administrative assistant, Miss Marilyn R. Ender.

Any errors that remain are my own.

E.H.D.

TABLE OF CONTENTS

# INTRODUCTION

There is a new interest in the work of Thomas
Reid. To cite only a few examples of this recent
interest, two journals, The Monist (Vol. 61, No. 2
for April, 1978) and Philosophical Monographs (Vol. 3
for 1976), have devoted special issues to his work.
Norman Daniels has a book on Reid: Thomas Reid's
'Inquiry': the Geometry of Visibles and the Case
for Realism (New York: Burt Franklin, 1974), and
the various journals of philosophy have more of such
materials appearing monthly. Reid's own major works
are once again readily available and some of his
works are being published for the first time, e.g.
his Lectures on the Fine Arts, recently transcribed
by Peter Kivy (The Hague: Martinus Nijhoff, 1973).
There was an early edition of his Philosophical Orations published in 1937. The Orations were delivered
by Reid, in Latin, at the graduation exercises at
King's College, Aberdeen, between 1753-1762. It is
my understanding that the 1937 edition was also in
Latin, but, at any rate, these have now been translated (by Shirley M. L. Darcus) and edited (by D.
D. Todd) for the Philosophy Research Archives (June,
1977). The special issue of Philosophical Monographs
has an extensive bibliography which is expanded and
updated in The Monist.

One can only speculate on the reasons for this
renewal of interest. Two reasons seem obvious.
First, David Hume died in 1776. Thus, in 1976, there
was a lot of interest among philosophers in the "Hume
Bicentennial". Observances, with addresses by world-
famous philosophers and the publishing of commemora-
tive volumes, were held in Edinburgh and at McGill

University in Montreal.  Many journals published
special issues, and a number of new books appeared
devoted to philosophy of David Hume.  But philosophical discussion is rarely simple, unalloyed praise;
it is critical.  And those who seek to criticize
Hume soon discover that, in his own time, Hume's
major critics were his fellow Scots, members of a
group known as the "Scottish philosophers of Common
Sense".  This group included George Campbell and
James Beattie, but its outstanding spokesman was
Thomas Reid.  Thus a study of Hume leads almost inevitably to a study of Reid.

     As every citizen of the United States knows,
1776 was also the year the American Colonies de-
clared their independence from Great Britian.  What
is not so well known is that some of the more prom-
inent signers of the Declaration were Scots, e.g.
John Witherspoon and James Wilson.  And many of
those who were not Scots themselves were taught by
Scots; we need only instance Benjamin Rush and Thomas Jefferson.  The Scottish Philosophy was, as I
have argued elsewhere, extremely popular in early
America from the College of New Jersey (which later
became Princeton) in the colonial period to Baylor
University at its first location at Independence,
Texas in the middle nineteenth century.  It was a
no-nonsense philosophy, opposed to skepticism--in
faith and morals as well as epistemology--and it
was a philosophy which placed a low priority on abstract, obscure, metaphysical'thought.  In short,
the American Bicentennial led to renewed interest in
American philosophy and its history, and this, once
more, meant renewed interest in the Scottish Philosophy of Common Sense and the work of Thomas Reid.
Finally, those who, for whatever reason, look into
the books written by Thomas Reid, will find in them
much of lasting philosophical value.

     No attempt will be made here to give a detailed
biography of Reid, or a thorough analysis of his
work.  James McCosh, who was President of Princeton
University in the third quarter of the nineteenth
century, included a biographical account of Reid's
life and work in his The Scottish Philosophy, which

is available in a recent reprint edition (Hildesheim: Georg Olms, 1966). The account by McCosh was based on the earlier "Account of the Life and Writings of Thomas Reid, D.D." by Dugald Stewart, which was included in Sir William Hamilton's edition of Reid's collected works (Edinburgh: James Thin, eighth edition, 1895). By rather general agreement, the best philosophical analysis of Reid's work is The Scottish Philosophy of Common Sense by S. A. Grave (Westport, Connecticut: Greenwood Press, 1973).

Having cited the best biographies and the best philosophical analysis, the present writer may be excused for being brief, and even for oversimplifying difficult philosophical issues. To be specific, Thomas Reid was born in 1710 and died in 1796. He was born in Strachan, Scotland, near Aberdeen, and attended Marischal College. There he was trained for the ministry, and served as a Presbyterian pastor for several years. He also served, for four years, as a librarian at Marischal. It is difficult to understand just why he was chosen for the post, but in 1751 Reid changed his role from preacher to professor--at King's College, Aberdeen.

Two comments must be made regarding Reid's years in Aberdeen. First, he preferred the system then in use at King's College, called "regenting". In this system, one teacher would lead a group of young students through their entire four years of college. He taught them everything--all subjects in the curriculum, though of course, any given professor would be better qualified in some areas than in others. Also, while in Aberdeen, Reid helped form the Aberdeen Philosophical Society, with Beattie, Campbell, Alexander Gerard, and others. The members met to eat, drink, and to discuss philosophical papers. Both McCosh and Stewart note that Reid's papers, read before this Society, formed the content of his first major work, his Inquiry into the Human Mind on the Principles of Common Sense, which he published in 1764. That same year, 1764, Reid moved to the University of Glasgow to become Professor of Moral Philosophy there, replacing Adam Smith. In 1780, he retired from teaching to put his thoughts in order

xiii

for two more books, largely gleaned from his lectures, Essays on the Intellectual Powers of Man
(1785) and Essays on the Active Powers of Man (1788).

Reid's thought is not easily summarized, but,
more than anything else, he opposed skepticism--es-
pecially the skepticism of David Hume. Reid thought
that there are some things that we just know; it's
foolish to deny that. We know that we exist, that
we have minds, bodies, etc. If anyone denies these
things, there's no hope for him, because he is beyond the reach of human reason. We know that some
things are morally bad, others good, though we may
argue about which is which. Reid often spoke of
"basic principles of our nature", implanted in us
by the "Author of our nature". God has made us so
that we cannot really doubt that we exist, that we
have bodies, etc. If we say we do doubt these
things, this must be some sort of philosophic ploy
--or else we must be sick. Again, to be brief, an
appealing aspect of Reid's work is his interest in
ordinary language. For example (and there are many),
in his work on ethics he notes (in opposition to
Hobbes) that acting for our own interest is one
thing; acting for the sake of duty is quite another.

An obvious difficulty with Reid's method is
that his disciples (and perhaps Reid himself) can
sometimes go too far. If we think that we can learn
from the dictates of common sense, how far does this
go? In James Oswald's An Appeal to Common Sense in
Behalf of Religion (1766) and James Beattie's On the
Nature and Immutability of Truth (1770), it extended
to hurling insults at Hume while reciting pious
platitudes.

But to return to Thomas Reid, a study of the
lectures he gave in 1780, his last year of teaching,
reveals that there is more that should be published.
I first saw those lectures, in xeroxed hand-written
copies, in 1974. That year, I was given a "Summer
Sabbatical" to go to Scotland to do library work.
At the University of Edinburgh Library, I asked to
see Reid's lectures, and was shown a three-volume
set of Notes From Dr. Reid's Lectures (listed as

Phot. 1211); these are xeroxes of originals found in the Mitchell Library, Glasgow. The text was difficult to read, but, again, I thought I found material that was not in Reid's published works. I spoke with Prof. George Davie of the University of Edinburgh, a recognized authority in this area. He agreed that there was much in the lectures that should be published. Specifically, he agreed that Reid's criticisms of Adam Smith's moral philosophy had not been published, and should be. I also noted that the lectures have a series on "Natural Theology" which had not been published. Accordingly, I had xeroxes made of the reply to Adam Smith and the series on Natural Theology, and obtained permission to publish from the Mitchell Library, Glasgow. I transcribed what I could decipher (as best I could make it out) of the lectures on Smith. Then I added a historical introduction to them. But I had never lectured on Adam Smith, so I turned the transcribed material over to my colleague, Prof. Robert M. Baird, and asked him to supply "Critical Comments". The entire package was published as "Thomas Reid's Criticisms of Adam Smith's Theory of the Moral Sentiments", in the Journal of the History of Ideas (Vol. XXXVIII, July-September, 1977).

In 1977, I was able to get another sabbatical (for eight months) to begin the work of transcribing the lectures devoted to "Natural Theology", which begin with Lecture 73, dated February 11, 1780, and are continued through Lecture 87, dated March 3, 1780.

It is important, as it turns out, to be as clear (and as honest) as possible about just what we have here. When I first went to Scotland in '74, I was naive. I assumed that the lecture notes were written by Thomas Reid himself, in his own hand. I think (now) that the title, Notes From Dr. Reid's Lectures, should have been a clue (but it wasn't) that this might not be the case. My faith was shaken by a paper by David Fate Norton, in which he criticized Kivy's work on Reid: ". . . but Professor Kivy apparently failed to notice that the manuscript with which he was working . . . is not in Reid's hand, nor does he seem to have compared this manuscript (which may well have been dictated by Reid) with the many other important manuscript materials on the same subject which were written by Reid."[1]

To be very personal for a moment, those words filled me with two conflicting concerns. Had I also made a mistake with the Reid lectures on Adam Smith? If so, I didn't want my colleague Baird involved. It was important to me to state clearly that it was never part of his task to determine the authenticity of the lectures. But, on the other hand, I could not help thinking the parentheses rather absurd ". . . (which may well have been dictated by Reid) . . ."!?! If that's true, why should it matter whether or not they are in Reid's "own hand"?

Further, I learned that the practice in Scottish universities in those days was that the professor read his lectures, much the same lectures year after year. Anyone who has lectured to bright students for any length of time would be able to predict that, at least the second or third time around, the students would have their own copies. Thus in the biography of one of Reid's colleagues at Glasgow, the great professor of Law, John Millar, we read:

Following all but universal practice, no doubt with examinations in mind, students would take more or less full notes on the professor's lectures--in most cases in long-hand, with the usual improvised shorthand, but in some cases quite clearly in a regular short-hand. Often these notes would then be transcribed and written out more fully at the student's leisure--in some cases, it would appear, to be sold to other students.[2]

It is a matter of record that the Rev. Hugh Blair, who lectured on rhetoric at the University of Edinburgh, claimed that one reason he had his Lectures on Rhetoric and Belles Lettres published in 1783 was that his students already had their

own copies, and even bought them at the local book-
stores. So what's wrong with student notes? Obvi-
ously, there could be a great deal wrong with them.
The lecture notes could be fragmentary and incom-
plete. This is not the case with the notes of Reid's
lectures of 1780. Or they could be garbled and/or
simply misunderstood by a sleepy or dull student.
I can find no such cases in the lectures on "Natural
Theology" (though there may be some). The few that
have been found in the lectures on Adam Smith may
be my fault; I think I've gotten better at reading
eighteenth-century script. But I have found not a
single case in which the student notes (if such they
are) could lead to serious philosophical misunder-
standing.

        This whole matter is of concern to me because
Prof. Norton was kind enough to send me a manuscript
(which he co-authored with Charles Stewart-Robert-
son), in which my colleague Baird and I are given
the same treatment he had earlier given Prof. Kivy.
The paper was sent, he wrote, so that if we found
"anything offensive or exaggerated", we could let
him know "in time to attempt a modification". In
fact, the paper had already been sent to the Journal
of the History of Ideas before it reached us, and
is scheduled for publication in 1980 or '81. At one
point in the paper Norton and Robertson say:

        To be sure, the text erroneously published
        under Reid's name corresponds sufficiently
        with his own text to allow one to give it
        a high place among the known student tran-
        scriptions of Reid's lectures; indeed to
        the editors of Reid's own lecture notes,
        this student transcription is a valuable
        aid in the placement of fragmentary texts
        within the larger pieces left by Reid.
        But a serviceable index is at best a poor
        substitute for an authentic work. . . .

        This is not the place to defend my paper on
Reid and Smith; that can be done at another time.
But, clearly, the relevance of all of this is that
the same sort of remarks could be made of Reid's

lectures on "Natural Theology". So let us say, for
the sake of argument, that the lectures published
here are student notes, and not in Reid's own hand.
I do not think that they (or the Smith papers) are
therefore "erroneously published under Reid's name".
They have too much in common with Reid's published
works and other unpublished manuscripts for that to
be the case--and what, exactly, is the "error" here?
At any rate, Norton is working with seven boxes of
"Birkwood Manuscripts" in the Library of Kings College, Aberdeen. These are the "authentic" works to
which he refers above, which are, he assures us, in
Reid's own hand. For my own part, I am content if
my efforts can serve as a "valuable aid" to the understanding of the work of Thomas Reid. This is not
the first "serviceable index" that I've produced.
In his paper in Philosophical Monographs, Norton
lists in "very general terms" the contents of the
Birkwood Manuscripts. It is worth noting that he
does not list any manuscripts on natural theology.
But I have not personally examined the Birkwood
Manuscripts, and it is possible that Norton includes
such lectures under some larger topic. If not, the
lectures in the Mitchell Library in Glasgow would
have a much greater value than that of serving as
a "serviceable index" to those in Aberdeen.

If we are clear, and honest, this question of
whether or not the lectures are in Reid's own hand
may not be all that important. Many of the works
of Adam Smith (and of Aristotle, Epictetus, etc.)
exist largely as student notes, but scholars are
pleased to have them. In our own day, how much
would we have of the thought of Wittgenstein were
it not for the notes taken by his students (and
their efforts in dealing with his own unedited
notes)? Of course, we should always seek something
better. It is therefore to be hoped that Norton's
work in Aberdeen will yield valuable results. But
to leave all this aside, what value can be claimed
for the lectures published here for the first time,
and why have they never been published before?

The best answer to the first question may be
that Thomas Reid, after almost a century of relative

neglect, is at last emerging as a major figure in eighteenth century thought. And these lectures help to "fill out", so to speak, the picture we have of the man and his work. For example, harking back to his period of regenting, they reveal that Reid had a truly amazing command of such diverse fields as human anatomy, botany, astronomy, and mathematics. Beyond that, the reader will, very candidly, find few major surprises. For example, the careful reader of Reid's published works will not be surprized to learn that he is attracted to the "design" argument for the existence of God, the sort of argument used later (in 1802) by William Paley in his Natural Theology. This careful reader will recall that Reid had written in his Essays on the Intellectual Powers of Man, "When we attend to the marks of good contrivance which appear in the works of God, every discovery we make in the constitution of the material or intellectual system becomes a hymn of praise to the great Creator and Governor of the world."[3]

The argument from design is developed at some length in the lectures on "Natural Theology".

Similarly, there is a short Chapter (Chapter XI of Essay IV) on the subject "Of the Permission of Evil" in the Essays on the Active Powers of the Human Mind in which Reid wrote, "The defenders of necessity, to reconcile it to the principles of theism, find themselves obliged to give up all the moral attributes of God, excepting that of goodness, or a desire to produce happiness."[4] In the lectures there are lengthy discussions of the moral attributes of God, and of the problem of evil, and the argument is levelled against Leibniz that he makes God good at the expense of making Him just. The reader will also find many other interesting philosophical arguments in the lectures. To cite only one example, Hume claimed in his essays that the design argument would, if it worked, lead to a concept of a finite God. The reason, Hume argued, is that we have a right (a logical or intellectual right) to infer in a cause only as much wisdom as we find displayed in the effect. But, Reid replies in the lectures (my paraphrase here) if we heard a

great scholar lecture for an hour (dazzling bril-
liance!), would we be inclined to say "Well, that's
all he knows." Wouldn't it be strange to say that?
In general, Reid, in the lectures, fills out (again)
and gives more detailed analyses of relevant topics
only touched upon in the two books he published after 1780.

There is a haunting sentence at the end of
Reid's essay on the permission of evil and before
the shift to ethics in Essay V, "Of Morals" (it is
to be noted that in the lectures, Reid also moved
next, after "Natural Theology", to "Ethics"). Reid
wrote, "Bishop Butler, in his Analogy, has an excellent chapter upon the opinion of necessity, considered as influencing practice, which I think highly
deserving the consideration of those who are inclined to that opinion."5 This is as if to say,
"If you care about natural theology, I suggest Jo-
seph Butler, Analogy of Religion (1736); it's good
on that." Indeed, it is a good book, used and re-
spected in schools across Great Britain and America
(including Baylor University at Independence) for
most of the eighteenth and nineteenth centuries--
but why didn't Reid publish his own lectures on the
subject? Reid admired Butler on ethics, too, but
he published his own book. Why didn't he publish
the lectures on natural theology? I shall suggest
three possibilities:
        (1) They weren't his.
        (2) Reid was "nervous" about religion.
        (3) He did not consider the lectures worthy of
publication.

The first is, I readily admit, a bit of wild
speculation. But it is known that Adam Smith lectured on rhetoric and belles lettres in Edinburgh
before moving on to Glasgow and that he passed his
lecture notes on to the Rev. Hugh Blair. Blair
acknowledges this and admits having used them. I
believe a comparison of the published student notes
of Smith's lectures and Blair's Lectures on Rhetoric
and Belles Lettres will show that Blair really did
use them, and to advantage. It is just possible
that the same happened with Reid. We know (from

Stewart's account of Smith) that Adam Smith lectured
on natural theology at Glasgow before Reid. Could
he have followed his earlier precedent and left his
lectures to Reid? There are no extant copies of
Smith on natural theology, not even student notes.
I am not suggesting that Reid simply read Smith's
lectures, in the way that, as a young preacher, he
had read to his congregation the sermons of Tillotson. Some of the ideas found in the lectures would
have repelled Smith, and there are references to
books (e.g., d'Holbach's System de la Nature) which
were published long after Smith had left Glasgow.
What is possible is that Reid used Smith's work to
supplement his own so that, after sixteen years of
lecturing, he was unable to disentangle them. But
this is wild speculation, somewhat akin to the postulates that Lord Russell once said had all the advantages of theft over honest toil.

The second possibility is more likely, i.e.
that Reid was "nervous" about religion. It should
be recalled that the Church of Scotland, which produced such scholars as the historian William Robertson, Hume's close friend Robert Wallace (Malthus'
Principles of Population was, at least in part, a
reply to Wallace's Dissertation on the Numbers of
Mankind, 1753) and Hugh Blair, also produced John
Knox, John Witherspoon and John Cairns. The last
three were not noted for their tolerance and understanding toward those having differing religious
views. In Reid's youth, he must have known about
the continuing battle that another professor at
Glasgow, Francis Hutcheson (along with his friend
William Leechman, who remained at the school well
into Reid's tenure there) had had to fight against
immoderate factions in the Church. He knew that
David Hume had failed to get a university teaching
position. George Davie's book, The Democratic Intellect: Scotland and her Universities in the
Nineteenth Century (University of Edinburgh Press,
1961), is a careful record of the struggle that
led to the great loss of prestige of Scottish philosophy, in the nineteenth century, at the hands of
fundamental extremists such as John Cairns. It is
sometimes noted that Reid had much in common with

Immanuel Kant. Neither led very exciting lives.
Both wrote their major works late in life. It should
be remembered that when Kant's Religion within the
Limits of Reason Alone drew official censure, he qui-
etly withdrew it at once. Reid's lectures on natural
theology may seem to us to be innocent enough. But
at the very start he says, if I may substitute current terms, that revelation cannot go it alone. It
needs to be supplemented with rational (philosophical?) analysis. To quote from his first lecture on
"Natural Theology", "It is no doubt true that Revelation exhibits all the truths of Natural Religion, but
it is no less true that reason must be employed to
judge of that revelation, whether it comes from God."
Cairns certainly, and probably Witherspoon, would
have thought this a damnable heresy. I have heard
major Scottish philosophers say that Reid was "nervous" about the possibility of problems with the
Church, and I believe this to be true.

Finally, Reid may simply have thought that his
lectures on natural theology were unworthy of publication. Once more, Dugald Stewart's "Account" of
Reid's life is instructive, and there is a passage
in it that must be quoted at length:

> His opinions on the most important
> subjects are to be found in his works, and
> that spirit of piety which animated every
> part of his conduct forms the best comment
> on their practical tendency. In the state
> in which he found the philosophical world,
> he believed that his talents could not be
> so usefully employed as in combating the
> schemes of those who aimed at the complete
> subversion of religion, both natural and
> revealed; convinced with Dr. Clarke that,
> "as Christianity presupposes the truth of
> Natural Religion, whatever tends to dis-
> credit the latter must have a proportion-
> ately greater effect in weakening the au-
> thority of the forever." In his views of
> both, he seems to have coincided nearly
> with Bishop Butler, an author whom he held
> in the highest estimation.[6]

Thomas Reid was a modest man, very uncertain of his own abilities. Stewart suggests that had he not had the approval of his friends in the Aberdeen Philosophical Society, he would have published little or nothing. And he had great admiration for Butler; perhaps he did feel that he could not improve on what Butler had done. But, again, this is speculation, at least until more of Reid's manuscripts on Butler are published. It is more important to ask: regardless of what Reid thought, are the lectures in fact worthy of publication? I think I've said enough to show where I stand, but this is a matter that each reader must decide for himself. The quotation from Stewart points, I think, to another consideration that makes their publication important. That is the fact that Reid was, first and foremost, a religious thinker. There are some figures in the history of thought who may or may not have been religious; this seems to have no bearing on their philosophies. But this is not the case with Thomas Reid. His faith was important to him, as a man and as a philosopher, and this faith is nowhere more prominently displayed than in the lectures on natural theology. Thus they reveal the man more truly and more completely than any of his other works, and may also be an extremely "valuable aid" toward an understanding of his thought as well.

Elmer H. Duncan

# ENDNOTES for INTRODUCTION

[1]David Fate Norton, "Reid's Abstract of the Inquiry Into the Human Mind", Philosophical Monographs, no. 3 (1976), p. 125.

[2]William C. Lehmann, John Millar of Glasgow, 1735-1801 (New York: Arno Press, 1979), p. 23.

[3]Thomas Reid, Essays on the Intellectual Powers of Man (Cambridge, Massachusetts: The M.I.T. Press, 1969), p. 668.

[4]Thomas Reid, Essays on the Active Powers of the Human Mind (Cambridge, Massachusetts: The M.I.T. Press, 1969), p. 350.

[5]Ibid., p. 359.

[6]Stewart's "Account" is included in The Works of Thomas Reid, edited by Sir William Hamilton (Edinburgh: James Thin, 1895). The quote is to be found on p. 32.

# REID: FIRST PRINCIPLES AND REASON
## IN THE LECTURES ON NATURAL THEOLOGY

In 1764, Thomas Reid became professor of moral philosophy at the University of Glasgow, succeeding Adam Smith. In that same year, he published his An Inquiry into the Human Mind on the Principles of Common Sense. The thought within the Inquiry appears to have been seminal to much of the thought found within the lectures he gave at Glasgow. This same thought is very apparent in his lectures concerning natural theology begun on February 11th and concluded on March 3rd in the year 1780, his final year as professor of moral philosophy.

This paper will concern itself with Reid's notion of "first principles" and his application of this notion to natural theology. It is the intention of this paper to show the intimate relationship which holds between the common sense principles and the reasoning process of Reid's natural theology, and that the inevitable limitations of common sense epistemology must also be limitations for Reid's proofs for the existence and attributes of God. The material concerning the natural theology will be based primarily on Reid's lectures, numbered 73 through 87, recently transcribed by Dr. Elmer H. Duncan, Baylor University.

I shall first attempt an elaboration of the principles of common sense as posited by Reid. I will clarify what I regard as a mistaken view of an aspect of the subject which R. E. Beanblossom advocates in his "Introduction" to Thomas Reid's Inquiry and Essays, 1975. In this discussion, I will note

with Beanblossom that there is a close tie between
Reid's argument for the existence of other minds
(intelligences and wills) and his version of the
argument from design for the existence of God.
This version of the design argument is meant, in
part, to be an answer to the skepticism of Hume,
and to Hume's criticism of natural theology.

It is very important to note that Thomas Reid
does not discard reason as a philosophical tool
merely because he espouses the principles of common sense as a basis for reasoning and for knowledge. Indeed, Reid relies heavily upon reasoning
from these principles, as axioms, for his argument
for other minds as well as for his argument for the
existence of God and for his answer to the problem
of evil. I shall conclude with a brief discussion
of this latter problem.

## 1. First Principles and the Problem of Other Minds

In order to come to terms with the notion of
first principles, one might look briefly at the notion of natural signs. Natural signs, as opposed
to artificial signs which are determined by habit
and custom, are the effect of the constitution of
the human mind. For Reid, signs suggest to the
mind certain conceptions. For instance, the artificial sign "gold", because of custom and habit,
suggests a conception of gold. Likewise, certain
natural signs, such as the sensation of hardness,
because of the original constitution of the human
mind, suggest certain conceptions, such as the conception of hardness and a belief in that conception.
Because of our constitution, we have a propensity
to leap from natural signs to a belief in the suggested concept. The connection between our sensations and the conception and belief of external
existences is taken to be "an original principle
of human nature."[1]

What we view here in Reid's work is a reliance
upon the "original constitution" of the human mind.

Such a reliance is found in many of the British Empiricists, including David Hume. This "original constitution" is the basis for what Reid calls "common sense". There are certain "common sense" beliefs to which human beings naturally hold because of the human psychological constitution. A belief in the material world is an instance of such common sense beliefs.

Baruch Brody notes the importance of the human constitution to this type of thinking in his article "Hume, Reid and Kant on Causality." An underlying consideration in the theories of causality presented by each of these three philosophers is that "one has to take into account constitutive facts about the human intellect in developing a theory of causality."[2]

Brody also postulates, however, that despite this point of unity in the three theories, the conflict between Hume and Reid (and Kant) is still present, specifically with regard to the relevance of the facts about human psychology to epistemology. That this is true becomes clear if we look at Reid's Inquiry and the conception there of philosophy.

It is a thesis of Reid's that reason has for too long been divorced from common sense. This is a fault he finds with Hume. Indeed, the conclusions Hume reaches are very different from those one might reach by way of the beliefs natural to us as humans.

For Reid, reason and common sense "have both one Author."[3] If we may doubt the latter, may we not also doubt the former? For reason to be possible, one must admit something which is not proved by reason alone. Even Hume accepts a belief in the existence of impressions and ideas which is not supported by reason any more than is a belief in the existence of minds and bodies.

"All reasoning," says Reid, "must be from first principles. . . ."[4] And if reason does not help as the servant of common sense, "she must be her slave."[5] In such thinking, Reid attempts to reconcile common sense and reason by basing reason on common sense.

Thus he proposes what he calls the "first principles" of common sense.

We see, then, that although both Hume and Reid espouse a view of the uniformity of the human psychology--a view that there are current features naturally inherent in the constitution of human beings--a difference between them lies in the fact that Hume tends to divorce reason from common sense, whereas Reid seeks to marry them.

Every man with a sound mind is a competent judge of the first principles of common sense; the few yield here to the many. In Essays on the Intellectual Powers of Man, Reid lists what he judges to be the common sense first principles which are the foundation of his epistemology and his natural theology. In order to provide a foundation for knowledge, these principles, as stated by Paul Vernier,

> must be non-inferentially justified and independently credible, else they fail to terminate the justification regress with which knowledge is otherwise threatened.[6]

The principles, then, are based upon the natural constitution of the mind (e.g., the propensity to leap from natural signs to a belief in the suggested concept).

All first principles answer three points of description. To begin with, as has been mentioned, every man is a competent judge of them; they are generally assented to by all men. Secondly, to hold an opinion which contradicts a first principle is not only to err, but to hold to an absurdity. Most important to my criticism of Beanblossom is a third point set forth in the following passage:

> It may be observed, that, although it is contrary to the nature of first principles to admit of direct or apodictical proof; yet there are certain ways of reasoning even about them, by which those that are just and solid may be confirmed,

and those that are false may be detected.[7]

In other words, the principles are beliefs held before we could reason; they are self-evident, yet we may still reason about them.

Despite the fact that all first principles may be described in the three ways indicated above, and despite the fact that they are all a part of the general human constitution, they may be divided into two types: the principles of necessary truths and the principles of contingent truths. Contingent truths in general are those which are mutable, and may be true at one time and false at another. The sun need not necessarily rise in the east. Beanblossom does not take this distinction seriously in his criticism of Reid's treatment of the problem of other minds.

Let us look at the problem of other minds. We will do so in order to further distinguish the importance of common sense principles, necessary and contingent, to the reasoning process. This will enable us to better understand the contribution Reid makes to natural theology.

In any epistemology, the problem arises concerning the existence of other minds. How do we know that our fellow human beings are intelligent, thinking, willing beings and not automatons? Some answer that we can never know, others seek to define intelligence and will in terms of effects (behavior). Both answers have their inevitable consequences, good and bad. Reid, interestingly enough, tends toward a synthesis of the two.

If knowledge of other minds means something other than a common sense belief in the existence of other minds, then he cannot help but side with the skeptic. We must depend, he holds, upon such a common sense belief (that other humans are living and intelligent) if we are to escape skepticism.

Reid presents this belief as a common sense principle of a contingent truth. He lists the principle as the belief "That there is life and intelligence in our fellow-men with whom we converse."[8] The principle does not rest on the foundations of reasoning, it is one to which we adhere long before we stop to reflect upon philosophical matters. Yet, Reid goes on to provide a reason for this belief should we set aside our natural conviction. The reason he provides rests on the necessary first principle stated in the Lectures as the belief that from the marks of design and wisdom one may infer intelligence in the cause.[9] Thus it is that Reid adopts the second part of his synthesis, discussed above. Intelligence is inferred naturally from the signs of intelligence present in the behavior of other humans. We deduce that certain signs are signs of intelligence and design by way of a comparison with our own behavior.

Now, if I understand Beanblossom correctly, he complains that as Reid provides a form of reasoning to justify the belief in other minds, and the belief in others as free agents, he also "contradicts what he has said about first principles in general and the first principles of morals in particular."[10] Beanblossom holds that Reid rejects his own argument that a self-evident belief cannot be proven true by attempting "proofs" of first principles.

This criticism seems to hold specifically for Reid's "common sense" belief that man possesses moral liberty. Indeed, Reid discusses three arguments of "proof". But does Reid intend by these arguments to prove a first principle? Reid tells us merely that these arguments to prove that man possesses moral liberty are the ones "which have the greatest weight" with him.[11] As is noted in the arguments, the mere fact that this principle is a common sense belief actually throws the burden of proof upon those who would deny it. Still, there is no reason why rational arguments may not be applied in support of the principle. As we have indicated, Reid does not wish to divorce either reason from common sense, or common sense from reason.

Though it is not clear, it appears as though Beanblossom holds that Reid also seeks a "proof" of

the existence of other minds, because he must prove
the existence of God. The claim made is that here
Reid also contradicts what he has said about first
principles. But as we have seen, Reid does not re-
ject his doctrine that first principles cannot be
directly proven. He notes, rather, that reasoning
cannot be effectively applied against the beliefs,
unless these beliefs are not common sense principles.
Reason can be applied, however, in support of the
principles. This appears to be particularly true
of contingent truths. Says Reid,

> Thus, the belief we have, that the per-
> sons about us are living and intelligent
> beings, is a belief for which, perhaps,
> we can give some reason, when we are
> able to reason; but we had this belief
> before we could reason, and before we
> could learn it by instruction. It seems,
> therefore, to be an immediate effect of
> our constitution.[12]

It is not Reid's intention to divorce reason
and common sense. Rather, common sense principles
provide the basis for reason. This does not mean
that reasoning cannot be applied to these principles.
Certainly, no principle is capable of complete proof
by reason, but it is capable of having reason applied in support of it.

The principle that our fellow-men have intelligence and life can be, at least practically, deduced from other principles. Part of what makes it
itself a first principle is the fact that reason
alone cannot prove it in any complete sense, and
that we hold it as a belief prior to any reasoning.

Now, it may appear that we have wandered quite
astray from our topic. Actually we are very near
it. As is pointed out by Beanblossom, Reid attempts
a justification, by reason, of the belief in the intelligence and free will of other finite beings, because he must apply such a justification to the
Deity. Beanblossom notes that nowhere does Reid
list a belief in God as a first principle.

Reid cannot do so for several reasons. It is not a belief which is self-evident, nor is it assented to by all men. Reid can reason to the existence of God in the very same way in which he reasons toward the existence of other minds. This does not mean, however, that he can make the former into a common sense principle of contingent truth, as he does the latter. For one reason, a contingent truth may be true at one time, and not at another. This would provide little basis for a belief in God.

Since the belief in God is not a common sense belief, it seems, it can be proved or disproved by reason. It is my intention to question this at a later time. Reid's hope is to prove the existence of God by way of a deduction from common sense principles. If we adopt the argument form which we utilize in arguing to the existence of other minds, we run into problems.

Before we look at Reid's Lectures, let us first briefly recapitulate what we have thus far accomplished. We noted that principles of common sense are based in the original constitution of our minds. This fact in itself, according to Reid, lends them credibility for epistemology. Thus it is that Reid can use them as axioms for the foundation of reason. This does not mean, we noted, that we cannot reason about these axioms. Indeed, Reid does just that (remaining consistent with what he argues concerning the nature of first principles). Specifically, he looks at the belief in other minds. The form of reasoning he utilizes to reach this belief is precisely the form that he uses in proving the existence of God.

## 2. Reid's Natural Theology

There are many significant arguments to be found in Reid's lectures on natural theology. I shall here, however, confine myself to a study of the issue of common sense principles within natural theology, an issue which I believe to be the most significant aspect of Reid's lectures.

True to the cause of natural theology, Reid holds that revelation should not hinder reason, but should help it. It is only by reason, indeed, that we can tell what is a true revelation, and what this revelation might mean.

Reason, for Reid and for others of his time, is a means for achieving a solid theological system. But it is also the case that reasoning which is falsely grounded can lead us astray, not only from common sense, but also from the truths of religion. I have previously noted that one criticism which Reid wields against Hume is that Hume does indeed divorce reason from common sense and, in doing so, formulates some practical absurdities. Likewise, Reid criticizes Hume for not grounding his approach to theology in common sense.

It is Reid's intent to ground reason in common sense principles. There are two of these principles, in particular, that are vital to his natural theology.

The first principle which is very important to his theology is listed again as a metaphysical principle of necessary truth in the Intellectual Powers: "That whatever begins to exist, must have a cause which produced it."[13] This principle is the ground for Reid's version of the cosmological or First Cause argument.

It is absurd to say that a chain (no matter how many links it has) is supported from above by nothing. Likewise, if one views a file of blind men (each with a hand on the shoulder of the one in front) which is so long that the leader cannot be seen, one still believes that there is a leader. We, as humans, have a natural propensity, because of our constitution, to infer support for the chain and a leader for the blind men. In a similar fashion, all things which exist we naturally assume to be the effects of a cause. This is the case even if we are discussing the universe, which stretches back in time so far that we cannot see its beginning. This, the argument that there is a necessary first cause, is grounded in a common sense principle.

Reid might agree here with the skeptical view
that we cannot rationally demonstrate in any conclusive way the <u>necessary</u> existence of any being. But
this must be taken to be true in the same sense in
which it is impossible to conclusively prove any
first principle. The first principles, as parts of
human nature, are the axioms for reasoning, not the
end product.

Reid says,

> This argument then from the present exis-
> tence of things to an eternal cause of
> all existence seems to be grounded on the
> plainest principles of reasoning and
> there is no exception made to it which
> can bear examination.[14]

Throughout his work, Reid explicates the ambi-
guity of the word "cause". In the <u>Active Powers</u>,
he notes that its "original and proper meaning" is
lost in the crowd of the many meanings the word has
been assigned. A sailor may consider the cause of
the motion of the needle of a compass to be the mag-
net he moves back and forth before it. A Cartesian
philosopher "pities the ignorance of the sailor"
and concludes that the cause is "magnetic effluvia,
or subtile matter."[15] A Newtonian philosopher, of
<u>course</u>, confesses his ignorance of the real cause
and proceeds to describe what he can observe, in
terms of natural laws. At any rate, none of these
can point out the real efficient cause of any phenomenon within natural philosophy. Even the laws
of nature are not, in themselves, the efficient
causes of anything. They are really the rules according to which the effects are produced. "The
rules of navigation never navigated a ship; the
rules of architecture never built a house."[16]

If whatever begins to exist must have a cause,
it also appears that this cause has certain qualities which we can discern. According to Reid, it
is shocking to common sense to think that inanimate
and senseless matter might confer sense, reason and
intelligence to created creatures. It would seem,

then, that the First Cause would possess not only existence but also life, power and intelligence. A cause must have the power to produce the effect, as well as the will to do so.

This is tied in with Reid's assumption of a second principle of common sense which is important to his theology. This principle has been mentioned before as the natural inference from marks of design and wisdom in the effect to intelligence in the cause. It has been seen that this principle is important to Reid's argument concerning the existence of other minds. It is also a key premise in his argument for the existence of God from design, or the argument from final causes.

The argument from final causes is reduced by Reid to the following syllogism: 1. "an intelligent first cause may be inferred from marks of wisdom in the effects." 2. "There are clear marks of wisdom and design on the works of Nature," therefore: "the works of Nature are effects of a designing and wise cause."[17]

The first premise is the obvious result of the all-important common sense consideration. A man's wisdom is known by its effects and the signs of it in his conduct. Likewise, we cannot see "bravery", but only the effects of that bravery. From these effects, as signs--natural and artificial--our minds take the leap toward the inference of their cause. Thus we pronounce the wise man wise by way of his conduct, the idiot an idiot by way of his. When we see the marks of intelligence and wisdom in another human being, we infer that he has intelligence and wisdom. Likewise, if we take the popular example of finding a watch, we may infer an intelligent creative force, and a designer, behind the watch.

This principle can neither be proved by reason nor derived from experience. Hutchinson attempted a justification of the principle by way of reason but, although Reid admires the work of Hutchinson, Reid believes that the attempt was doomed by its nature to be unsuccessful. Even philosophers who reason excellently must simply rely on the common sense of Mankind when regarding the question of the justification of inferences toward other intelligences.

Likewise, the first principle is a necessary principle and thus cannot be derived from experience, unlike the belief that the sun always rises in the East and sets in the West which is a contingent belief, depending "on the will of the Maker of the World."[18] Indeed, when we concern ourselves with beliefs such as that of the sun always rising in the East, we find that experience tells us only of what has been and what is, not of what shall be. It may show a conjunction of event A with event B, but can never show a necessary connection.

The principle that from the intelligence found in the effects, one may infer the presence of intelligence in the cause is a necessary principle in the same sense that the rule "twice three makes six" is necessary, independent of experience.

The second premise of Reid's syllogism must be taken as true or false through observation. As with others who adopt the argument from Design, Reid spends much time looking at nature in order to demonstrate that design and purpose are evident in the universe. His approach differs slightly from the classic look at nature found in Paley's Natural Theology. Reid is less concerned with the amazing ways beings physically fit into the environment and the astounding intricacy of such things as human anatomy, and is more concerned to note that things in the Universe are beneficial to man's own designs and purposes. This is not to say that he discards the observations which one such as Paley might make. Indeed, these are very much incorporated into his work. I would suggest merely that the difference between the two approaches is one of emphasis. In Reid, there seems to be much more of a stress on things in the universe being fit for Man's use.

Let us take an example. Both Paley (some years after these lectures) and Reid recognize that the universe is regulated by certain principles and, as Reid notes, the workings of a watch are incomparable to the perfect workings of "the Planetary System in which wisdom and design so clearly appear."[19] Anything which might appear to be an imperfection is seen to be so because we, as humans, are still ignorant concerning certain aspects of nature. A disruption in the universe is not a perfect design foiled, but must be seen as the natural consequences of a God working through natural laws.

Both Paley and Reid recognize that the stars are fixed in certain ways in the sky. Reid, however, continues from here to infer that they are fixed for certain purposes congenial to the actions of men. Navigation, for example, is possible because of the stars.

Likewise, for Reid, the earth is well suited for its inhabitants. He suggests that some might ask the purpose of oceans, then, and why oceans are not productive fields. One of Reid's answers to this question is that the ocean is necessary to supply rivers with water. Another answer, just as basic to Reid, is that oceans enable us to realize the possibility of navigation by which we may visit other lands. Because of this possibility, the world has seen its great civilizations, and their commerce, grow along the seas.

Another question he suggests one might ask concerns why there should be mountains rather than plains in some areas. Mountains, replies Reid, contain precious metals, minerals and other resources which are important to man. He sees mountains as cellars for these metals and minerals.

Though he does look at the sign of design and wisdom in the structure and adaptation of animals, even here it appears he is most interested in those signs which are beneficial to man's purpose. He says,

Tis evident that some of the animals are intended for the use of others to serve them as prey, but still more were intended for the use of men. The ox was intended to assist him in his laborious employments, the horse the dog and the Elephant were all designed for the service of Man and they have generally such instincts as fit them for this purpose.[20]

Overall, however, Reid's intention is the same as Paley's. In looking at the structure of the human body, Reid notes that Galileo, who was brought up on the Epicurean tenets of a "fortuitous concourse of atoms" and the tenet that there is no providence[21] was converted to a belief in the existence of a Designer when looking at the structure of the Body. This effect is one sought by those who defend the second premise of the argument from Design. (A further discussion of design in the human mind and society is found in the 78th Lecture.)

The conclusion of Reid's syllogism is that the works of Nature are effects of a wise, intelligent, designing cause. The conclusion is derived from the premise based upon common sense and the premise based upon observation. It is this form of syllogism which, as we have suggested, Reid applies to the problem of the intelligence of other human beings. Yet there is a major difference which is not noted by Reid.

Reid tells us that whoever denies the syllogism for the argument from final causes also denies "the existence of any intelligent being but himself."[22] One has the same evidence in nature for the wisdom and intelligence of God as he does for that of the wisdom and intelligence of his fellow human beings. In both cases, an inference is made from characteristics of observed effects to characteristics of the cause which must remain unobserved.

In the problem of other minds, however, we noted that reason cannot prove in any final way that other human figures possess intelligence or life. The belief in other minds is justified because it is a first principle of common sense. It is justified because it is rooted, as are other such first principles, in the constitution of the human mind. Reasoning toward this first principle, as we have noted, can provide no proof for it. Its "proof" lies entirely in the fact that it is a principle of common sense.

So, despite the fact that the argument form is the same for both the problem of the intelligence of other people and the problem of the intelligence of God, there is present between the two a very large discrepancy, which remains undelineated by Reid. The difference is this: In the first problem, our conclusion derives its final validity not from reason but directly from common sense, whereas, in the latter, our conclusion concerning the Designer rests entirely upon the reasoning based in common sense.

Where then is the proof of a designer? If we insist that the final proof is provided for by way of a reasoning process which rests on a common sense principle, then must we not also admit that a final proof of the intelligence of finite beings around us is possible by way of this same reasoning process? But this is to contradict what Reid has said about the nature of first principles. This, as I take it, is Beanblossom's assertion.

Rather, we might argue that Reid may logically be required to provide proof through reason for a belief in an intelligence behind nature simply because this belief is not a first principle. Reid cannot provide a final proof for the belief in the intelligence of other finite beings because this is a first principle, fulfilling all the requirements for such a first principle. He may justify by reason the claim that it is a first principle, but he cannot provide a final proof for it. This does not mean that the same reasoning process (from common sense principles) cannot provide a final proof for another belief which is not a first principle.

But, how valid is any method of reasoning from common sense principles? As we have said previously, Reid considers those principles to be first principles which are within the natural constitution of the human mind. Is the truth or falsity of a first principle to be decided by way of its being or not being originally or naturally constitutive of the human mind? It seems that to say first principles are a part of the constitution of human nature is merely to make a description.

It would appear that to reason from such principles towards the proof of anything must be, by necessity, to limit the investigation to the realm of the powers of the human, especially the human common sense. The "certainty" in the proof of, say, the existence of God, rests upon the constitution of the human mind. We cannot escape a reasoning relative to common sense in order to find any non-relative, absolute truth. All our reasonings and investigations are necessarily tempered by the prejudices of our nature. We could only know the absolute truth of, e.g., the conclusion that there is an intelligent and wise first cause, if we could show that the principles of common sense are themselves true in some absolute sense, or in a sense of a correspondence between human experience and the way things "really are." This we cannot do. We can only hold to a common sense belief that things are the way we hold them to be. It appears as if we do not avoid P. Vernier's threat of an unending justification regress in any fashion that admits of any absolute truth. We only avoid such a regress if we accept the constitution of our own minds as a limiting factor to our knowing processes. This is basically agreed to by Reid and constitutes a major difference between himself and Hume. Ironically, however, the Professor of Moral Philosophy cannot provide any absolute justification for the absolute issues he wishes to deal with.

What do we have then? Even if we are to accept the possibility that we may definitively prove the existence of an intelligent and wise cause because a belief in such an intelligent cause is not a common

sense belief, we must still base that proof on common sense belief. But where is the justification
for common sense beliefs? That justification, Reid
might argue, can be found primarily in the fact that
common sense beliefs are rooted in the human constitution. This, I would suggest, might prove a justification for the holding of certain beliefs (because
we can't help but do so), but it cannot provide a
demonstration for any of these beliefs themselves.
In other words; it cannot be a "proof" of any sort
that any of these beliefs hold true in any absolute
manner.

### 3. The Attributes of God and the Problem of Evil

We have thus far shown that because Reid mar-
ries Reason to common sense, he necessarily accepts
the prejudices of the human constitution which must
limit the certainty and truth of any conclusions
reached by reasoning. This means that certainty
must always be relative to our own condition. Any
certainty which we might call "absolute" must be a
certainty "absolute" only given the limitations and
boundaries of human knowledge.

Reid admits that we cannot know, because of our
limited capacities, many of the attributes of God.
He says:

When we consider attentively the works of
Nature we see clear indications of power,
wisdom, and goodness, yet we see still
much remains into which we cannot penetrate and of which we must be forever ignorant. If this is true then in this
case, may it not be expected that our notions of the great author of all will be
imperfect and inadequate as our notions
of his works. The divine Nature indeed
is a more proper object for the humble
veneration of the pious heart than of
curious disquisition to the most elevated
Understanding.[23]

He notes further that we have no means of forming conceptions which are to any degree adequate to
the object, the Supreme Being, we deal with. We can,
then, form a conception of the Supreme Being only
when we have some analogous conception of such attributes in ourselves. Perhaps, there are attributes
of the Deity which we can never know, just as a blind
man can never see colors.

Reid, however, would suggest we can know certain
attributes of the Deity. We can infer the existence
of certain attributes from their appearance in the
operations of Nature. We can also reason toward certain divine attributes from the fact of his necessary
existence. Likewise, if we should ascribe to the
Deity every perfection, we may argue from these unlimited perfections.

Reasoning toward attributes of the Deity by way
of his necessary existence and unlimited perfections
is as important to Reid as is the reasoning toward
attributes from their existence in Nature. This constitutes his reply to David Hume's claim that "we
ought to ascribe to the Deity no higher degree of
wisdom and goodness"[24] than is to be observed in his
limited, imperfect works. A cause is, according to
this view, exactly proportional to its effect.

This, says Reid, may be true of natural causes,
but not of causes which are intelligent and voluntary. Hume's argument depends upon the supposition
that no attribute may be inferred from anything but
the existence of the observable effects. This, according to Reid, is simply absurd. When one asks a
person for directions to Edinburgh, and receives
them, one does not infer that the directions given
constitute the whole of that person's personality
and intelligence. Reid claims that the attributes
derived by reasoning from the Deity's necessary existence and unlimited perfections should possess a
great deal of force in the argument for the existence
of those attributes in the Deity. Because Hume ig-
nores these, he tends to lessen the perfection of the
Deity, reduce his attributes from the infinite to the
finite level, and also tends to compare the human

excellencies to the excellency of God. "Shocking thought!" cries Reid, "Presumptious man! does think with the short line of thy understanding to search the unfathomable wisdom of God?"[25] Reid criticizes the impiety and pride of such an idea and borders on ad hominem when he says:

> Indeed the idea is so singular, that I
> once imagined that either Mr. Hume or
> his Epicurean friend must have been the
> inventors of it, but I find that Milton,
> long before Hume's time, has attributed
> it to Lucifer, who gives the same reason
> to encourage his associates to rebellion
> against their Maker but they were con-
> vinced of their error by this event.[26]

But perhaps Reid himself must be accused of pride, for he is very certain of a reasoning process which, based on human common sense, determines the attributes of the Deity. We may reason from, for example, the principle that God has a necessary existence. But this principle rests upon common sense, a natural part of our constitution. The reasoning rests, then, both upon our strengths and limitations.

Reasoning in this way, however, Reid discerns certain natural attributes of the Deity, including duration, immensity, unlimited power, spirituality and so forth . . . , as well as moral attributes including goodness and forbearance, truth and veracity, a love of Virtue and a dislike of Vice, and justice and equity. Because of his attribution of such moral characteristics to God, Reid can bring a new twist to answering the traditional problem of Evil.

Under this system, the problem of Evil does not necessarily run contrary to the purposes of God, as it seems to do with Leibniz's system.

For Leibniz, the universe is constructed so that the greatest degree of good may be attained on the whole. But Leibniz, despite his intentions, is, according to Reid, a part of a misguiding tendency in theology to reduce all of the Deity's moral attributes to benevolence. This tendency is made particularly evident in Boyce's pamphlet Divine Benevolence. This made the problem of Evil particularly potent, and oftentimes evil was shrugged off as a necessary part in the system.

Reid contends that goodness or benevolence alone is not enough to make a perfect moral character, in Man or God. He also contends that evil should not be seen as necessary or fatal or as something which cannot be removed by Divine power.

He goes on to discuss different types of evil and their causes: the evil of imperfections which cannot be avoided; natural evils which are the result of accidents conforming to natural and general laws (e.g., houses may fall because of gravity), and which are necessary to the training of men in wisdom and prudence; and moral evils which are not caused by God but by the abusive use of the will of free agents (who are given their free will by God).

Reid provides an answer to the problem of evil by insisting that there are attributes of the Deity aside from those of benevolence and goodness. These attributes provide good reason for the occurrence of different types of evil. For example, God likes Virtue and virtue must be developed in men by way of their reactions to problems in the world.

But, once again, we run into the problem of the limited knowledge of man. Surely, we can reason about the attributes of God, but we must do so from common sense. In doing this, we can never escape the prejudices of our own minds. Practically or pragmatically, this may not be a problem. Indeed from a pragmatic point of view it might seem absurd to suggest such a problem. But in dealing with a problem such as the existence of God, one might ask for absolute answers rather than merely relative ones. Reid can only provide answers from a base of the common sense of man, answers relative to human nature. The ascription of attributes to

the Deity, and the answer to the problem of Evil
provided by Reid must necessarily be human answers
with limited certainty. Whether or not this is
the case for those who assume that their systems
are based upon first principles considered in any
way absolute or ultimately true is the basis for
lengthy philosophical investigation.

We have attempted to show the intimate connection in Reid's work between common sense and
Reason. We indicated that common sense principles are a part of the original constitution of
the human mind and are in this way independently
credible and non-inferentially justified. But if
reason is based upon these principles, it is limited to conclusions which accept the limitations
of human knowledge. Epistemologically, it would
appear that we know things only on a common sense
level with a type of practical certainty, rather
than any "absolute" certainty. Thus, when Reid
moves to a proof of the existence of God, to a
proof of the attributes of God or to an answer to
the problem of evil, and he does so by way of a
reason based upon common sense, we find that his
conclusions must be limited in this fashion. This
problem might be remedied by a suggestion or attempt to prove that common sense principles are
universal to all intelligences and true with or
without the human element. Whether or not this
is in any way possible or even feasible, I should
not conjecture. But, if Reid makes any such attempt, it is not stated explicitly.

If Reid were to suggest, as others have, that
common sense principles may be taken to be universally true because they are God-given, then it would
appear that a vicious circle could not be avoided.
This would hardly be a satisfactory answer to the
problem.

This epistemological problem of the limits
and restrictions of human knowledge is hardly uni-
que to Reid for it is a problem with any system
that asks after the nature of knowledge. This is
particularly so with theoretical systems derived

by reason. It is a problem with David Hume as much as it is a problem with Reid. And it is certainly a problem for all those who attempt "natural theologies" of the sort set forth by Paley, Bishop Butler --and Thomas Reid.


William R. Eakin



ENDNOTES for Essay


[1]Thomas Reid's Inquiry and Essays, edited by Keith Lehrer and R. E. Beanblossom (Indianapolis: Bobbs-Merrill Co., Inc., 1975), p. 44.

[2]Baruch Brody, "Hume, Reid and Kant on Causality," in Thomas Reid: Critical Interpretations, edited by Stephen F. Barker and Tom L. Beauchamp (Philadelphia: Philosophical Monographs, University City Science Center, 1976), p. 12.

[3]Inquiry, p. 53.

[4]Ibid., p. 57.

[5]Ibid., p. 54.

[6]Paul Vernier, "Thomas Reid on the Foundations of Knowledge and his Answer to Skepticism," in Thomas Reid: Critical Interpretations, p. 14.

[7]Inquiry, p. 260.

[8]Ibid., pp. 277-278.

[9]Thomas Reid, "Lectures on Natural Theology," transcribed by Elmer H. Duncan, Baylor University, 1980, p. 54.

[10]R. E. Beanblossom, "Introduction," in _Thomas Reid's Inquiry and Essays_, p. xxxvi.

[11]_Inquiry_, p. 336.

[12]Ibid., p. 265.

[13]Ibid., p. 290. Also, "Lectures," p. 10.

[14]"Lectures," p. 14.

[15]_Inquiry_, pp. 311-312.

[16]Ibid., p. 313.

[17]"Lectures," p. 54.

[18]Ibid., p. 53.

[19]Ibid., p. 21.

[20]Ibid., p. 34.

[21]Ibid., p. 42.

[22]Ibid., p. 56.

[23]Ibid., p. 61.

[24]Ibid., p. 63.

[25]Ibid., p. 94.

[26]Ibid.

# Natural Theology

Lect. 7th Feby. 15. 1780

Of all the animals which God has made
it is the prerogative of man of Man to know his Maker. There
is no kind of knowledge that tends so much to elevate
the Mind as the knowledge of God. Duty to God forms an
important part of our duty and is the author of every Virtue; it gives us magnanimity, fortitude & tranquillity, & answers unto ease in the most adverse circumstances; and there can be no rational piety without
just notions of the perfections and providence of God. It
is no doubt true that Revelation exhibits us the truths
of Natural Religion, but it is no less true that reason
must be employed to judge of that revelation, whether
it comes from God. Both are great lights given to us
by the Father of light & we ought not to shut out the
one in order to use the other. Revelation is of use
to enlighten us with regard to the use of Natural
Religion, as one Man may enlighten another in
....things

xxxxviii

# NATURAL THEOLOGY

## Lect. 73$^d$
### Febr. 11, 1780

Of all the animals which God has made it is
the prerogative of Man alone to know his Maker.
There is no kind of knowledge that tends so much
to elevate the Mind as the knowledge of God.  Duty
to God forms an important part of our duty and it
is the support of every virtue; it gives us magnanimity, fortitude and tranquility; it inspires with
hope in the most adverse circumstances, and there
can be no rational piety without just notions of
the perfections and providence of God.  It is no
doubt true that Revelation exhibits all the truths
of Natural Religion, but it is no less true that
reason must be employed to judge of that revelation; whether it comes from God.  Both are great
lights and we ought not to put out the one in order
to use the other.  Revelation is of use to enlight-
en us with regard to the use of Natural Religion,
as one Man may enlighten another in things that it
was impossible could be discovered by him, it is
easy then to conceive that God could enlighten Man.
And that he has done so is evident from a comparison of the doctrines of Scripture with the systems
of the most refined heathens.  We acknowledge then
that men are indebted to revelation in the matter
of Natural Religion but this is no reason why we
should not also use our reason here.  Revelation
was given us not to hinder the exercise of our reasoning powers but to aid and assist them.  Tis by
reason that we must judge whether that Revelation
be really so; Tis by reason that we must judge of
the meaning of what is revealed; and it is by Reason

1

that we must guard against any impious, inconsistent or absurd interpretation of that revelation. As the best things may be abused so when we lay aside the exercise of reason Revelation becomes the tool of low Superstition or of wild fanaticism and that man is best prepared for the study and practice of the revealed Religion who has previously acquired just Sentiments of the Natural. The best notions of the divine Maker which we can form are imperfect and inadequate and are all drawn from what we know of our own Mind. We cannot form an idea of any attribute intellectual or moral as belonging to the deity, of which there is not some faint resemblance or image in ourselves. As we cannot form the least conception of Material objects but must somehow or other resemble those we perceive by our senses so our knowledge of Deity is grounded on our knowledge of the human Mind. And for this reason I thought it best to give you a view of it before we entered upon this subject. In speaking of Natural Religion I shall adopt the plan which has been followed by Mr. Hutchinson in a tract which he has published and which I shall take this opportunity of recommending to your attention and careful perusal.[1] The first branch is to treat of the Existence of God and of his Nature and attributes and of his Works.

1. The existence of The Supreme Being is so loudly proclaimed by everything in Heaven and Earth, by the structure of our bodies and the no less curious structure of our Minds and indeed by everything about us, that it may perhaps appear unnecessary to confirm a truth so evident. But when we consider the importance and that there have not been wanting persons who have exercised their uses to weaken its evidence, it will appear proper to consider the grounds on which it is supported and to enquire into the forces of the sophistical arguments that have been urged against it. I shall therefore point out some observations that appear to have the greatest strength in confirming the important truth I shall first however offer a few remarks on the causes of speculative Atheism and consider if it can justly be drawn from this system that there is no God.

2

I conceive then that there are chiefly 2 causes that may be assigned for the Speculative Atheism that has appeared in the world. There were a few among the antients that professed atheism as Diagoras, Theodorus and Protagoras and in later times we are told that Julius Caesar Varinus[2] suffered death for atheism in the dark ages. What seems to have led them to embrace their opinion may, as I said be ascribed to two causes.

1. to false systems of philosophy by which they thought to account for the formation of the World and what happens in it without once bringing in a wise and intelligent maker. They conceive that by a mixture of moisture and drought the mighty machine of the Universe was provided without any intelligence to begin, regulate or finish its operation. The philosophers of the Ionic School were generally thought to lean to Atheism, because that philosophy was chiefly employed in accounting for the formation of the universe. Everything arose from chaos by a mixture of the elements and we find that Anaxagoras was the first who thought it necessary to introduce Mind into the system and who thought intelligence necessary to put all things in order. All other antients who differ from Anaxagoras much either hold that the world existed from all eternity without a cause or was produced without an intelligent cause and author. The ignorance of true philosophy which leads men to discern marks of wisdom and design in the formation and government of things may be considered then as one cause of Speculative Atheism.

But,
2. It was intended by some to free mens minds from the fear of punishment for their crimes in an after state to free them from all reflections on the future or remorse for the past. Epicurus who does not deny the existence of God, but thinks he does not interest himself in the affairs of the World, glories in this as a great benefit done to all Mankind, that he had freed them from the fears of Religion and all the evils which a dread of the Gods never fail to create. Lucretius celebrates

3

his praises on this account and by all his colleagues he was also reckoned a kind of deity, who had
nobly delivered them from the bugbears of Religion.
He seems to have taken it for granted that as
there was no Supreme Being, that therefore there
was no future life, nothing after death, neither
rewards for Virtue nor punishment for vice and of
consequence they might pursue their pleasures without any restraint. This was the conclusion, supposing the principle true, which they drew but I
conceive that these men have reasoned ill even on
the principles of Atheism and before I enter on the
arguments in proof of the existence of deity, let
us consider the conclusions that follow from this
system of Atheism and whether other conclusions
justly can be drawn from it, on account of which
it seems to have been adopted by some. It is indeed difficult to reason on a hypothesis so absurd,
but let us for a moment suppose that Heaven and
Earth are either from all eternity without any
cause or even produced by chance without the interposition of any intelligent power. Suppose then
that this is the case will it follow from thence,
1. that men must perish at death and that there
is no further existence. 2. That if there is a
future life that it will have no relation to the
present and that our happiness and misery in it
will not depend on our conduct here. 3. Whether
it would tend to make us happier in the present
life, if there no God, no future state, and all
things governed by unalterable laws, man under the
preservation of a universal ruler who governed all
things wisely and well. These it may be proper to
consider a little and see whether they may justly
be deduced from the principles of Atheism or not.

1. There is no Supreme Being, therefore there
is no future state and men must perish at death.
Now to me there does not appear the least shadow of
connection between the two propositions. If our
present existence is consistent with his non-exis-
tence why not a future? that the thinking principle
is distinct from the Body which we see and feel has
already been proved by convincing arguments, then
whatever that principle is, let us suppose it produced by Necessity or Fate or any other unmeaning

4

name you please to give it, why may not that Chance
which at first united the organs disunite them? We
see other unions broken which appear equally strict,
as that between the Mother and the Child, the Egg
and the Mind. Thus it appears that even on the
principles of atheism there is not the shadow of
evidence for the position, we may grant the premise
yet the conclusion will not follow. But further--
we may observe that in the whole course of Nature
we have no proof of the annihilation of any one substance that exists. All the operations of Nature
consist either of the composition or decomposition
of what already exists without either creation or
annihilation. But the Soul is a subtile single
principle and therefore can perish only by annihilation of which we have no evidence in all Nature &
it cannot reasonably then be supposed in this instance. This argument is equally strong even on
the supposition of Atheism because it is drawn only
from what we observe of the course of Nature. We
may observe, too, that it is agreeable to the Analogy of Nature that we should pass thru different
states as different from one another as the present
from the future. Neither is this grounded on the
supposition of a deity but retains its full force
even allows the principle of Atheism to be true. We
see then that the Atheist cannot solace himself in
this conclusion, that because there is no God therefore there is no future state:  he reasons ill even
from the principles of Atheism.

        2.  The next conclusion I numbered was if there
is a future state will it have no relation to the
present and will our happiness or misery there not
depend on our conduct here?  And here again I maintain that this will not follow.  We have already
seen that granting the principles of Atheism to be
true yet we cannot conclude from them that the Soul
will not exist after death.  We have seen that there
are no good arguments against a future state, nay
that there are some arguments in proof of it which
retain their force even on the supposition of Atheism being just.  Let us now then suppose a future
state without any Supreme intelligent ruler, then
on that supposition let us enquire whether it is
certain that wicked men will not be miserable there

5

or if we will not find our good behavior here re-
bound to our happiness hereafter. I answer, that
it is neither certain nor probable that it will not
be so. Nor does any system of atheism furnish us
with any satisfying evidence that we will not reap
the fruit of our doings. Nay it is probable on the
contrary that we shall for, 1, Where animals pass
thro' different states, the future always has a connection with that which went before. Thus if a
chicken in the Egg receives any blemish it always
retains it and if it loses a foot or a wing it never
after recovers it. In like manner a child in the
womb if it brings any defect or disease along with
it, it continues thro' life and often renders its
days a few and evil. It is analogous then that we
should carry our good or bad habits along with us
to a future world. That vice is a disorder of the
Mind is as evident as that lameness is of the Body,
now, we have no evidence that it shall not be continued in a future as it is in a present life. The
excellence and superiority of temperance, prudence
and fortitude above their contrary vices is intrinsic and results from the Nature of Virtue and Vice
and we may as well suppose that twice three will
not make 6, as that there will be no distinction
between them here after. If therefore we reason
from analogy we see that there is a probability of
a good man's carrying along with him the fruit of
his virtuous improvements of his rational and moral
powers. These are his most valuable acquisitions
and if death doth not put a period to his existence
we have no reason to think that it will put a period to them. The vicious man has the same probability of feeling the consequences of his bad habits.
But, has the Epicurean any probability of finding
these objects to gratify his sensual pleasures? has
the votary of ambition any probability to hope that
his power will go along with him, or that there he
may raise himself to influence and gratify his lust
of dominion? or has the covetous man reason to
think that he will carry his idol along with him or
that he will draw bills of exchange of this World?
So it appears then, on the supposition of a future
state, even without a Supreme intelligent ruler,
that every probability promises happiness to the
Good and misery to the Wicked. We see that it is

in the course of things here and we can only judge of the future by the past. Were we to reason further on this subject, it would not be difficult to show, that whether we suppose the future world to be a social or solitary state, and if social, whether mixed of the good and the bad, or if we suppose the good and the bad separated, that in all of these cases still the chance is on the side of the Good. We have no reason then but to think that Virtue and Vice will always retain their Nature and produce their consequences. Let a man habituated to sloth and rapacity and injustice, change his climate or his country, let him live in regions of savage rudeness or in more polished society, let him leave even the converse of men and try the life of a hermit still will he find the bad effects of his habits follow him to the court or the camp, the city or the desert. From the Torrid to the Frozen zone he will find his habits noxious and sooner indeed may the Ethiopian change his skin than a man by altering his condition change his habits. What reason then has he to suppose that a passage to futurity shall wash away all his stains?

Thus have I showed that even supposing there was no God yet that this affords no argument against a future state, or why our conduct here should not affect our condition hereafter. I come to consider the

3. Conclusion, whether men would be happier in the present life if the belief of a God or a future state were removed or used as the impressions of a wise and righteous maker and governor of the World. I think it unfair here to compare as Mr. Bayle has done the consequences of Atheism with those of the worst kinds of Superstition[3], as I plead not the cause of Superstition but of Religion. Suppose it true, however, or suppose it may be, that these may create some notions even more pernicious than what will follow from Atheism. Yet this is not to the purpose. The abuse of the best things are always the worst. Men by abusing their reason depress themselves below the level of brutes. The abuse of meat and drinks is attended with hurtful consequences, so is it also with religion. I would compare the state

of men in a world conducted by inexorable fate,
with the condition of men living in a world governed by a righteous being, living under impressions
of a righteous administration of all things. And
I apprehend I need not say much to shew that the
former is more uncomfortable than the Latter. The
case of the world without a wise governor is like
a Ship without a pilot or a compass or any hand on
board who knew any thing about ships or sailing,
the winds and tides and currents drive her hither
and thither and she can pursue no determinate or
regular voyage. So on the system of the Atheist,
Necessity, or Fate, or Chance drive on everything
in the like blind way without either intelligence
or design. Nor would we not justly consider the
man as distracted who would choose to make a voyage in the former, rather than under the command
of an experienced master, and is not he equally
mad who can suppose that it would be better for
all men, that all events were directed by chance
than by an all wise Governor. Religion teaches us
to consider the Supreme Being as the kind father
of the Universe who knows our frame and teaches us
as a father doth his children. It is as bad then
to want to be from under his indulgent care, as if
children would wish to be orphans. But every man
is so far from this wish that he considers the existence of deity as as necessary to his well-being
as the Sun to the Planetary System. He rejoices
in a belief which is the Life of his Soul and the
spring of all his joys.

Men may be divided into two classes--the
Thinking and the Unthinking. Let us consider what
influence the belief of Atheism would have on each
of these.

As to thinking part of mankind--if they are
seduced into a belief of atheism, it would tend
only to plunge them into distress, anxiety and despair. He would see himself liable to many evils
which he could neither prevent nor remedy.--he
would see himself compressed with infirmities which
he could not remove--obnoxious to many dangers he
would not provide against--thus would misery present itself to him on every side and after all

often would some secret impressions of a Supreme Being, who would yet call him to account, come across his mind and enhance all his griefs. I do not deny that when in high Spirits and hurried away by the pleasing gales of prosperity he may banish remorse and all foreboding of futurity, but yet in his more serious moments when brought down by calamities to which all are liable, and especially when he has a near prospect of his dissolution, then all his thoughts let loose upon him and he is plunged into despair. If he could still retain his atheistical personality how would he rejoice in the thoughts of annihilation. But now he cannot enjoy even the comfort of this assurance.

As to the Unthinking again--the only effect it can have upon such is, to take away all restraint, to render him bolder in vice and callous to every manly feeling. All wise Legislators therefore have thought it proper to call in the idea of future justice as an adminicle to civil government. There is no example of any government where care has not been taken of the Religion of the Subjects. All governments have thought it necessary where any important affair depends on the testimony of witnesses that the religion of an oath should interpose as a proof of the truth of the declaration. All Princes and states too always confirm their treaties and contracts by the most solemn oaths. Such a general conviction of the Necessity of religion to aid the Civil government has led some to say that it was entirely a device of the Legislator and contrived by him merely the better to confirm his own authority and procure a ready obedience to his laws. This way of proceeding is at least a tacit confession of its utility.

Having said these things of the consequences that may be drawn from atheism and having shewed 1. that tho' there was no Supreme Being yet it does not follow that there is no future state, or 2. that our happiness or misery in a future state does not depend on our conduct here and 3. that even in the present life the belief of atheism has a worse effect upon our happiness than a persuasion that all things are governed by a wise and righteous governor;

9

I proceed now to offer some arguments for the existence of the Deity. Many of these have been given
by different authors, I shall give only those of
the most consequence, as I apprehend it is better
to offer a few of most force than to trouble you
with a great number.

1. Some authors have justly argued the necessity of a first cause from this, that everything
beginning to exist must have a cause. This principle I endeavored to shew you before was a first
principle; a principle to which all who are come
to years of understanding assent, and without which
we could not act with common prudence for a single
hour in life; a principle which was held as undis-
puted till Mr. Hume dared to doubt it, I had formerly occasion to consider his arguments and shall
not now resume what was then said. It is taken
for granted therefore.

What is either necessarily eternal without a
cause to produce it, or if it begin to exist, there
must be a cause of that existence; same being able
to produce it, and with regard to this being, it
too must either be eternal or if not then it must
have a cause to produce it, some other being with
power able to produce it. Thus we are necessarily
led to a first cause of all or to an infinite succession of beings, one producing another without a
cause. The last of these is evidently absurd; for
an infinity of beings without a first cause cannot
possibly be, because it would be a chain every link
of which would be an effect which stood in need of
a cause and what is true of a part is equally true
of the whole. Thus are we unavoidably led to admit
the existence of some eternal being, uncaused, necessarily existing and by his power producing everything we see.

ENDNOTES for Lect. 73<sup>d</sup>

[1]This is probably John Hutchinson (d. 1737) whose major work, Mases's Principia, was published in 1724.

[2]Could this be Lucilius Varini (1585-1619)?

[3]Pierre Bayle (1647-1706), Historical and Critical Dictionary, 1697, 1702.

Lect. 74<sup>th</sup>--

It is demonstrable then, that, if anything at all exists now, something must have existed from all eternity without a cause. For if we suppose there were two beings, let us call the one A and the other B, then if A created B, surely A could not be created by its own creature, and of consequence A must be without any cause to produce it, and the reasoning is the same if to these we add a third being or if we add three thousand or thrice thousand millions, still the same conclusion will hold. For there is no principle more evident than this that two things cannot mutually be the cause of each other.

Further--the same reasoning leads us to consider that which was uncaused, eternal and the cause of all other things, as possessed of Life, Power, and Intelligence. It is impossible that that which in itself hath neither life nor power nor intelligence should yet bestow them upon other beings. The same light of reason that convinces us that there can be no existence without a cause convinces us that every cause is not able to produce every effect. It is as shocking to Common Sense to say that mere inanimate senseless matter could confer sense and reason upon intelligent rational creatures as to say that things may begin to exist without a cause of that existence. I know only two ways which Atheists have taken to elude the force of this argument. The 1, is, By maintaining that the world as it now is existed from all eternity without any cause to produce it, or 2. By saying that there has been an eternal

13

succession of effects and causes without any first cause.

With regard to the 1. It has commonly been said, that it was maintained by Aristotle, however there are some doubts concerning this and his interpreters have followed different opinions, but we see that even those antients who reasoned bèst on the Atheistic system gave up this point. Epicurus and Democritus tho' they would not admit that the world was made by power and intelligence yet they acknowledged that it was not eternal. And we find Lucretius arguing strenuously against its eternity. Why, says he, if the world is eternal, why have we no monuments of any thing farther back than a few thousand years? Can we suppose that everything beyond that short period, short indeed when compared to eternity could have perished without leaving any vestige behind?

Tho' it is common to all nations to carry their history back to fabulous ages, thro' a pride of being reckoned the most antient, yet it is certain that we have no records that can pretend to any evidence that reach farther back than the Sacred Scriptures. The Chinese monuments the best attested beyond comparison of all others carry back their account of the history of their nation by Fohi hio[4] near the time of the deluge only, what goes beyond that is mere uncertainty without any evidence that can satisfy a reasonable men. Besides, it is evident in the things that we see that they are finite, dependent and changeable; one generation passeth away and another cometh. These things are sufficient to shew that the world is not eternal unless we suppose an eternal succession of effects and causes without a first cause which was the

2. Subterfuge of the Atheists I mentioned. But this evidently appears to be a great absurdity. The absurdity of it hath been illustrated by several authors in different ways. Thus, we may suppose a chain hanging down from heaven, composed of many links, the first of which we see

14

but lose sight of the last. Now were the question put, how is this chain supported? Would any man say, that the first was supported by the second, the second by the third and so on without end and yet that the whole was supported by nothing? Is not this absurd? It is as absurd, then, to suppose one thing produced by another and that by another and so on, because they all taken together make one great dependent whole and yet there is nothing left to create it--Another way of illustrating it is by supposing a file of blind men pass along, the last of whom had his hand on the shoulder of the one next to him, and his again upon the third and so on till we lost sight of them now were it asked, who leads them? All that we see are blind yet they keep the road distinctly and go on in a determinate path, and we would conclude from this that some person who sees leads the whole, but if any one will say, that every one leads another without the aid of direction of any seeing person, would we not see that the position was ridiculous and absurd. As well might we suppose that blindness multiplied a thousand times would make sight, that dependence multiplied would make independence, or a cipher a real number--This argument then from the present existence of things to an eternal cause of all existence seems to be grounded on the plainest principles of reasoning and there is no exception made to it which can bear examination.

The other topic from which proposed to argue the existence of a first cause or of a Deity was, from the appearance of wisdom and design which we see in the creation and in the Universe, to infer that they were at first produced and still are governed by a wise and intelligent cause. This is the argument which of all others makes the deepest impression on thinking men, and indeed it has this peculiar advantage that the more we learn by philosophical Investigation it thereby gathers strength, and every new discovery new evidences of the most excellent contrivance in the construction of things. When we are ignorant, we may often imagine that we perceive faults in the construction and management

of things, but this is the effect only of our ignorance, when we attend to them more narrowly and
perceive their uses more clearly what were thought
to be faults appear to be excellencies. Some have
conceived that the world would be more beautiful
if there were no mountains, if all were verdant
fields and flowery meads, and if there were no rivers or seas, but this is ridiculous; without mountains there would be no springs, without seas,
there would be no communication with distant coun-
trys or kingdoms, and we in consequence would always remain savages. And the same is the case
with respect to all others, what we think faults
in the constitution of the world is plainly an
evidence of our own ignorance. As therefore the
more we know the more we discover marks of wise
contrivance in the formation of the Universe. This
shows the importance of improvement in the knowledge of Nature, as we thereby bring more clearly
to light the great author of all. This is an argument which leads us to a very wide field, because
every object we can contemplate exhibits to us
marks of wisdom, and as it generally makes a deep
impression on men's minds I shall dwell upon a
little. I shall however mention only some of the
most obvious. I shall begin with those that are
most distant from us.

    The most distant objects which fall under our
view are the Fixed Stars. Their distance is such
that our imagination can hardly grasp it, yet we
find that they are not only ornamental but useful
to us who inhabit the globe of this Earth. That
we may form some conception of these bodies which
we call Fixed Stars it is proper to take notice
of some principles of astronomy. In reality philosophers have never yet accurately determined the
distance of the fixed stars; all that they have
done is to determine that it is not below such a
distance, but how much more they do not know. The
way in which they determine it is this, they can
determine the distance of the Sun and by comparing
the distance of the Sun with that of the Fixed
Stars they can thus form a kind of conjecture how
far distant they are. And till of late even the

distance of the Sun was not determined accurately, when by observing two transits of Venus, the one of which was in 61 the other in 69, they determined with certainty that the parallex of the Sun / i.e. the appearance of the Earth's semidiameter at the Sun / was not above 8'1/2" nor below 7'1/2"; this was made sufficiently accurate of innumerable observations of these two transits. From this by calculation on geometrical principles it was ascertained, that it must be 96 or 100,000 of miles. An amazing distance which Imagination is unable to grasp! But there is another means of proving this by the velocity of the rays of light, which pass to all objects on this Earth in a time imperceptible to us. Yet as all motion must (be) progressive it must take up some time and it has been proved to take between 7 and 8 minutes in its passage from the Sun to the Earth. But tho' the Sun is placed at such a vast distance yet are the fixed Stars inconceivably further. Such is their distance that viewed from them the semidiameter of the Earth's orbit will "seem only a point of a pen", so that they are distant from us millions of millions of miles, nor are we able to conclude that they are all at one and the same distance or what is their respective distances, for tho' they all appear to us placed in the surface of the same Concave Sphere yet this is owing to their being placed beyond the limits of distant vision, as we are not able to determine distances beyond a certain extent. It has been judged probable that them that appear least are only the more distant and not less, and that those of the brightest appearance and greatest apparent magnitude have this only from being nearer to us. That they may be placed at various distances thro' the immense void and are particular Suns illuminating other planetary worlds. But those which have the largest appearance and the most luminous are still millions of millions of miles distant from us. How unbounded the dominion of the Universal King who made and governs them all! But how amazed are we to find that these bodies placed at such a prodigious distance are yet useful to us; they are made perceivable to us by the little organ of the Eye

by means of the rays of light which move with such
velocity and are so minute that several of them
fall within the pupil of our Eye and are there re-
fracted so as to form an image of the Fixed Stars.
This amazing velocity of light whether considered
in the motion or the minisculeness of its particles
is no less wonderfull than the immense distances of
the bodies seen supplied by means of it.  But we
may (see) that the Fixed Stars are far from being
useless, they afford us light to travel both by sea
and land, by them the Heavens are marked out as it
were by fixed points; without them navigation never
would have been learned, without them Astronomy
never would have made any considerable progress.
Hence the use of the Fixed Stars to us does not
appear to be casual.  They were made not for the
sole purpose of glimmering faintly in a serene sky
upon this Earth, but they exhibit marks of wisdom
and design intending them for the most beneficial
purposes.


ENDNOTE for Lect. 74$^{th}$

[4]Manuscript unclear; could be Fu Hsi?

Lect. 75<sup>th</sup>

But in our own planetary system we perceive
still clearer marks of wisdom and design. It is
evident that the Sun being placed in the Centre
was intended to illuminate all the other planets
that move around him in different times indeed,
but observing the most regular order. The antient
Pythogoreans talked much of the harmony of the
Spheres, but had they known what is known now of
the harmonic motions of the Planets they would
have had much better grounds to talk on. It appears that their motions are regulated according
to the strictest mathematical rules which produces
a very great regularity, notwithstanding the law
of gravity, by which they act one upon another,
as well as are acted upon by the Sun. We know not,
for we have no means to know whether the power of
gravity by which the Sun retains all the Planets
in their orbits extends as far as the Fixed Stars;
perhaps they are placed beyond the sphere of their
power, or perhaps they are placed at such a great
distance that the effects of it are so much dimin-
ished that they will not be considerable while the
world lasts. But tho' we be ignorant of its power
over the Fixed Stars yet we know that it extends
to very great distances. It extends not only to
the Earth but to Saturn and not only to Saturn,
but likewise to all the comets belonging to this
system. All of which both planets and comets perform their revolutions in certain periods and in
regular orbits of an elliptical kind according to
certain rules which are common to all which were
discovered by the sagacious Kepler before the reason of them was known. He discovered that they

19

describe equal areas in equal times, and that their areas were proportional to their periodic times, that they all moved in ellipses of which the Sun was in one of their Foci, and he conjectured too that the square of the periodic times was in the same proportion as the cubes of the distances. This has since been found true by observation and it is wonderful how happy that philosopher was in guessing at properties of Nature but still the reason of all was unknown to him. The discovery of this was reserved for the great Newton. He observed that all bodies on this Earth gravitated to it, he observed that this power also not only reached to the tops of the highest mountains but even to the clouds by which they were prevented here entirely from us entirely falling from the Earth, now says he, why may not gravitation reach to the Moon; if it does to the Moon it may be that which retains him in his orbit. The general laws of motion had been discovered before his time. It had been discovered, that all bodies remain in a state of Motion or of rest till they be disturbed by an impelling force that change of Motion is proportional to the force, and to the direction of the force impressed, and also that there is a reaction contrary and equal to the impelling power. These laws had been discovered before but never applied to the power of gravitation but Newton found that the same Laws extend not only to the surface of the Earth but to all the Planets. It is evident from fact that this power decreases as you remove farther from the Earth. This has been found by experiment, because the motion of a pendulum is slower on top of high mountains than at the surface of the Earth. It appears that this power decreases in regular proportion as the distance of the bodies gravitating to one another increases and that it decreases reciprocally as the square of the distances. It is a power which belongs to all the planets. They gravitate to the Sun and the Sun to them, the Moon gravitates to the Earth and the Earth to the Moon as appears by the tides. The Secondarys of Saturn and Jupiter also gravitate to their primaries. Thus was this beautifull system carried on by this simple law and carried on

20

according to the exactest laws before the reasons
of them was known.  For Newton has demonstrated
that supposing this power to take place, then the
consequences would be, that this together with a
projectile force will make them describe elliptical curves, and that by this law they would describe equal areas in equal times and that the
square of the periodic times would be in proportion to the cubes of the distances.  Thus we see
the whole system regulated by exact mathematical
rules.  We see these producing the most accurate
and constant operations.  Now can we seek stronger
marks of wisdom and design than this?  If a man
sees the structure of a Watch and sees that the
whole is moved by one great spring; if he sees how
such wheels move such pinions which again move
other wheels and if he finds that--all of these
are regulated by the balance, would any man that
saw this pretend to say that it was the effect of
chance and produced without any skillfull agent?--
but what is this to the Planetary system in which
wisdom and design so clearly appear?--the Planets
of our system seem to have obtained their name from
their wandering appearance in their conjunctions,
oppositions, elongations, progressions, and retro-
gradations.  In all these cases they thought the
bodies of our system wandered while the Fixed Stars
seemed to remain in one plane but now men see all
these wanderings reduced to accurate rules and now
philosophers with the greatest east can predict
for 100 or (more) of years their precise plane and
various motions.  This was particularly seen in
the last transits of Venus over the Sun when she
appeared like a spot upon the Sun disk.  This had
been predicted by Kepler long before, but the
tables at that time were so inaccurate that even
Kepler himself began to doubt that it would not
happen yet an Englishman who had attended to the
Subject much was satisfied that it would happen
and had the happiness to see it.  Jeremy Horrocks
an Englishman in 1639 was the first of Adam's race
who ever observed this phenomenon.  We are sure
that it had not been observed before, because telescopes were not in use and without them it can't
be seen.  However his observations upon it were so

21

accurate that this transit can now be foretold and
has been seen since. I mention this only to show
by how accurate rules all the planets are regulated,
if they were not, it would be impossible to predict
their appearances, but these appearances are found
in fact and by experience to be regulated by un-
varying rules. Now chance acts by no rules; nothing regular is produced by chance. The learned
Archbishop Tillotson hath ever observed, as, by
throwing carelessly in a heap an infinite number
of types it is not to be expected that a fine polished poem would be made or even a tolerably sen-
sible discourse in prose, how much then can we suppose that this beautiful system of Nature could be
the work of blind chance owing to no fixed rules:
Nor does this power of Gravitation account only for
the comets and Planets in general keeping their orbits around the Sun but also for the irregularities
in the Moon's motion, for which the antient philosophers were obliged to invent so many cycles and
epicycles and which after all they could never
fully explain, but by the gravitation of the Earth
to the Moon accounts for it easily and fully. We
know not the number of comets belonging to our system but we know that they are regulated by certain
laws. These are so well known that some of their
appearances have been foretold. I have come accordingly to that prediction, that it is difficult
to determine it with accuracy till astronomy has
been accellerated for a long series of years. One
of them takes 75 years in its course and it observes its time exactly. Nothing then surely can
afford stronger marks of wisdom and contrivance
than our Planetary System. And if we descend to
the Earth we will perceive still stronger marks of
design there. The figure of the Earth as best for
various reasons is nearly spherical, not altogether
so, the parts at the Equator are higher than at the
poles and the figure becomes what is called an
oblate Spheroid. It commonly was thought to be an
exact Sphere, but were this the case then all the
parts towards the Equator would be overflowed with
Sea, the centrifugal bringing to the Equator from
the poles and leaving them dry. The wisdom of Nature appears here then in giving the Earth a figure

22

corresponding to the nature of this power, by which we see that these parts have all their just proportion of Sea and Land and so it is with all the Globe. We live too in an atmosphere surrounding the earth and which extends to 40 or 50 miles heighth above the surface of the Earth. This atmosphere was not made in vain. It is necessary both to animals and vegetables. Without breathing animals could not exist, even those that do not appear to have lungs yet all find air necessary, even fish could not live without air, and it appears equally necessary to vegetables as to animals and being thus necessary to all the wisdom of Nature hath produced it in sufficient quantity to answer all these purposes. It invests us around like our garments and we can go no where when we have it not. Some antient atheists have argued that it was useless, but without it we could have no rain; the vapour are carried up and supported by it, till they fall down by the action of gravity; and without it we would have no rivers, no springs. Thus we see all the constitution of Nature admirably fitted for the care of the various inhabitants of this Globe. Some antients also found fault too that there was so much sea, why was it not all fields, it thus supporting many more inhabitants? But in this we see the folly of Men when they begin to censure the works of God. We see it is necessary not only for furnishing supplies to rivers but also for Navigation. The wisdom of Nature intended us as Social creatures, and our Society was to be not only with those that are near but the most distant parts of the World and she therefore has furnished us with navigable rivers and with seas by which we may visit distant regions and convey their improvements and productions to our own country. No man can know the origin of Navigation; where seas are there nations have been found engaged in Commerce. And Commerce is one of the greatest means of improvement among Men. Hence as far back as we can trace antient history we find those the most improved who were soonest engaged in commerce. Thus all who lived on the banks of navigable rivers and of seas were always first civilized; first improved in arts and sciences, whereas those who inhabit the heart or inland parts of a Country

are long rude, thus in the heart of Asia and Africa
there has been no improvement for thousands of
years. On the other hand we see that the Egyptians
who lived on the banks of the Mediterranean the Red
Sea and the Nile were early a commercial people and
early flourished in the arts and Sciences. So too
the Arabians on the Red Sea, we see too the Chinese
have many navigable rivers and are a polished people. Surely then it is not in vain that Nature has
given such a great proportion of water. Thus antient atheists have thought too that mountains were
a useless deformity on the face of the Globe. Why
such rugged rocks and horrible precipices, the dens
often of wild beasts? Would it not be better and
more beautifull were it all a verdant plane? Here
too we see the uselessness of man in venturing to
censure the works of God. Were the Earth a plane
then there could be no rivers, because Rivers run
only where there is a descent. The springs fall
upon the laps of hills, where moistening the Earth
they descend till they come to some strata which
they cannot penetrate, they run along them and
bursting out, come down in copious streams. And
without rivers to moisten it how uncomfortable an ´
habitation would the Earth make! Besides--it is
evident that the mountains are fitted to maintain
some animals and so too vegetables of certain kinds
grow only on mountains. They contain also those
metals which are so usefull to Man and various sub-
stances from which human industry has reaped greatest advantages. Some pools indeed have introduced
metals, especially shining gold as the cause of
many evils to Man. However this may figure in
Poetry, there is no Truth in it, no solidity in it.
No doubt there have many evils arisen from the use
of it, but this is the abuse of the creations of
God, they tend to promote our advantage, but the
best things may be abused. And the placing these
minerals in mountains is a strong mark of design
and wisdom, as they are thus prevented from encum-
bering the face of the Earth. The great houses
thus are always cellars to hold what is not immediately usefull, so these may be called Cellars
for which to deposit the metals and minerals so
usefull to Man. No surely no man can call all this

24

the effect of chance or say that there is not wisdom
and contrivance in it.  Thus then we see evident
marks of design in the inanimate part of the Creator.
That part of the Creation which is unorganized &
hath neither animal nor vegetable Life, but if we
attend to the vegetable we find marks of wisdom
still more striking.  Vegetables differ from unorganized bodies in various respects.  In vegetables
there is some kind of organization to be seen and
all the parts of a plant have a certain relation to
the whole which is not discoverable in the minerals
and metals.  Thus a stone may be broken or divided
never so much but still each of these divisions is
a stone.  But with plants it is opposite.  They have
a certain unity by destroying which you destroy the
plant.  We do not know in what Vegetation consists.
We know indeed that every plant is filled with tubes
to carry up sap and that by this means the tree
gradually extends itself but how this effect is
produced it surpasses the power of Philosophy to
explain ----- ---- as yet.

The structure and organization of vegetables
is indeed wonderfull.  They bend their tender fi-
brous roots into the Earth and creep along in quest
of support, while the branches invariably ascend to
the light and flourish in the open air.  Besides it
has been discovered by some late botanists, that
many of the plants have what is called a Sleep, that
is, at certain times they shut themselves up as it
were to rest and at others they open their leaves
wide to receive the influence of the Sun and the
dew.  They are capable of an irritation by heat and
moisture, it appears by which they acquire life
whereas they are dead in the seeds.  These seeds it
is found can lie without life for a very long time,
sometimes for years and even for Centuries.  Yet
when they meet with a proper degree of moisture and
heat their powers disclose and they burst forth in
all their parts.  We know not what produces this
organization which distinguishes them from inanimate and bodies where the life is gone, far less do
we know how they grow and how they propogate their
kind, but we see that they are admirably fitted for
all these ends and that they are carried on by regular laws.  The variety of them is great but we evidently see the intention of Nature in giving that
variety corresponding to the variety of climate,
soil, heat and moisture.  Some we see atop the
mountains, some the valleys, some one season and
some another, one hot another cold, and by this
means is the face of the Earth always covered with
verdure and no soil is to be found without it, even
the rugged parts produce a great variety of beautifull and useful masses.  It appears to have been

27

the intention of Nature in this variety to satisfy
the uses and accomodation of Men and the inferior
animals. There is no Science which has been cul-
tivated with more assiduity in modern times than
Botany, yet the Botanist has not been able to as-
certain exactly the number of the various genera
of plants tho' to all probability they have been
fixed from the beginning of the World. We find
that this branch of knowledge was attended to by
the antients and so was carried to considerable
degrees of improvement by their labours.

Tho' in the days of Hippocrates it was in a
low state. But as their descriptions are so inaccurate, as hardly to be understood we are often
at a loss to know the plants by the description
they have given of it. Indeed the only description that can last and be understood by posterity
are those that are founded on some systematic and
accurate division and arrangement of the whole
genera and species, a plan which they never adopted.
This however has been adopted in modern times and
the descriptions now given are such as must be understood in all future ages. Future ages will thus
too be able to decide with more certainty whether
the same genera and species have always continued
or if any have been lost. But as far as we can
learn, it cannot be shewn that any one of them hath
perished or that any new one has been produced.
All of us seem to have been endowed with particular
qualities by the great Creator of producing each
after his kind, but none have a power of producing
new kinds. It is supposed that in all there may
be about 12 or 13 thousand genera of plants added
to our former stock on this subject by the late
discoveries in the South Sea. All of these have
distinct Natures by which they may be distinguished
from any others and may be described so as to be
known by the description. Now surely all this cannot be the Effect of Chance. They all observe established rules by which it appears that an all
wise cause first formed and still carries them on
in their operations. We see some of them fitted
for food to Man and the other animals, others for
Medicine, others for Cloathing. There is no use

of human life can be thought of for which some of
them are not properly fitted. And even those
plants which are poison to some are wholesome food
to others. Further--as they are the common aliment
of all, both men and brutes, for all either live on
vegetables or on some animals that are supported by
vegetables, it was proper that there should be such
a quantity as is sufficient to support the life of
all the inhabitants of the Earth and this accordingly nature has done. Some of them require no care
of ours in order to rear them, others again require
culture to bring them to perfection, and it evidently appears to have been an employment intended by
Nature for Man, that he should cultivate the various
plants of the Earth, discover their qualities and
fit them for his use; the first appearance of this
culture was in the Garden of Eden and it still continues an important employment to supply us with the
necessary supports of human life.

   Further they are all fitted with powers to
propogate their kind that none may perish. In ·he
manner of producing his seed and of disseminating
it we find a great variety. In some the seed is
strongly guarded by an oily coat, which defends it
[from] external injuries and admits moisture that
is sufficient for its growth but no more. Some of
them are wafted thro the air by down--others, are
thrown at a distance by the elastic spring of the
seed--some are carried by birds and so on. Some
of them we see are of a large, some of a small size.
How uncomfortable would life be without trees sufficient for houses, Ships and various utensils that
render life agreeable. As far back too as we can
have the history of men they appear to have used
some kinds of vegetables for Cloathing, as, flax,
hemp, etc. It may here be observed, that there is
in vegetables an unaccountable disposition, that
when the seed is planted in the Earth, whatever is
its position, still the roots push downwards and
the stems upward, but by what attraction or repul-
sion this is produced we cannot learn. We see that
in the seed there are two opposite ends from which
the stem and the roots open out, and yet tho' the
stem is placed downwards, yet it will turn round,

29

and pushes upward, on the other hand, tho' the roots be up, yet will they bend downward and search into the earth. Nay, we may observe that if a root is planted amidst earths of different kinds, its fibers spread around, avoiding the bad and seeking the best. Now we have no reason to ascribe to vegetables either sensation or thought, in this they are guided by the power implanted in them that is necessary to propogate their kind and provide against the species being lost. Neither are we able to explain the manner by which they derive their nourishment from the Earth, everyone drawing that which is proper to itself. For this purpose they have a wonderfully curious structure. Their roots are divided into very small fibers which receive the sap from the ground, which is conveyed in sap vessels, and is afterwards curiously altered and assimilated to the Nature of the plant by vessels of various kinds. This has been fully and accurately observed in modern times by Malpighi and Dr. Grew.[5] These two gentlemen formed the design of examining the structure of vegetables about the same [time]. Being both members of the Royal Society they transmitted their discoveries to them by whom they were published, and tho' they carried on their researches separately, yet their descriptions so remarkably agree as to add the greater authority to both. The engravings of these two philosophers shew that the works of Nature are continued at once in a beautiful and usefull manner. It may be observed--that particular parts manifest the intention with regard to the whole, now every intention supposes design and intelligence. Everyone sees that the roots are designed to furnish the plant with nourishment and to fix it firmly in the ground. The leaves also in time of a drought draw in moisture from the air. No man can doubt that the bark was intended for a covering to the tree and it serves admirably for this purpose, and the inmost bark is the part from which the growth arises, it being a film of the inmost bark that swells from year to year and marks an addition to the body of the tree. We see some of the seeds enclosed in a shell so hard that we can penetrate it with difficulty, we would be amiss to think then that it must rot in that shell, but Nature has

30

provided against this, for always opposite to that point from which the root opens it is so soft that the root itself is able to force a passage through it. Thus we see that Nature has provided against every difficulty, for that shell which to us seemed hardly penetrable is easily perforated by the slender fibre of a seed. Some plants too we see are not able to support themselves, they must be supported by other than, thus they cling to trees and walls whatever can bear them, of this kind are, ivy, vines and hops. For this peculiarity nature has provided in their structure, some of them are furnished with a kind of claspers which creep round the body that supports them, such are the hops and the vine. Others again exude from themselves a sort of dung which glues them to the body that bears them, as the ivy sticks to the rocks, and they adhere so firmly as to resist all the violence of the winds. It would be endless to mention all the marks of evidence and design which appear in the vegetable creation. What I have said may suffice to shew that they cannot be attributed to chance. I shall now consider a little the marks of wisdom to be seen in the animal creation. Here I shall divide what I have to say into three parts. 1. The marks of wisdom and design in the structure of the lower animals. 2. The structure of the human body. 3. In the human Mind.

In animals the equalities of both inanimate matter and vegetables join but they have something of a superior Nature to vegetation still. All of them have some perception of external objects and some of them too have a degree of Memory or something very like it, thus a horse, will know the way home again and will keep it even tho' it is so dark as that the rider himself should not know it. They appear too to have some trains of thought tho' we cannot discover their laws. We see among animals a great variety of different cases, each keeping the way prescribed to it by Nature. Some are viviparous and suckle their young, some again are oviparous and hatch their young by incubation. Yet all agree in breeding them carefully after they are produced.

By this Nature takes care that while the individuals are always perishing yet the species should
not entirely perish, accordingly in all the variety
we know of quadrapeds, of birds, of fishes, insects
and reptiles, it cannot be shewn that any one kind
has perished altogether. This however will be more
certain in future ages, because by the industry of
the moderns, they have been more accurately reduced
to genera and have been most distinctly described
by those who have applied to this branch of knowledge. It were to be wished that Natural historians
were more carefull in describing their various instincts. They have been laborious in describing
their structure, but surely the instincts by which
they live, and by which they are preserved and regulated are no less worthy of observation. These
have been more or less observed in every age. Aristotle has treated this subject; he made his collec-
tions and observations with candour and judgement,
being furnished with expenses by his pupil Alexander.
His descriptions are faithfull where he himself made
the observations, where he did not, he delivers it
only as a hearsay or report. The descriptions he
has given of what he saw are just and answer exactly
at this day. So true it is, that tho' man may in
several respects said to be not the same as in his
days, yet in brutes there is no difference, they
are the same now as in the days of Julius Caesar.
They are not able to communicate their knowledge
and for this cause never can arrive at higher degrees of perfection, but by instinct they are fitted to preserve themselves and to continue the
Species. And tho' some species are made the prey
of others yet we do not see that they ever perish,
Nature having made them more prolific in proportion
to the devastation made upon them. There is no
evidence that the brutes possess some of those
powers which distinguish human creatures as Abstrac-
tion, moral perception, reasoning, nor do they appear to have any power of Self government, they
seem to be always directed by what gives the strongest present impulse, nor do they appear to perceive
any rules of action to the attainment of any end.
It is true we see a kind of government among black
cattle, but they appear to be governed by instinct

32

rather than by final laws. And how prodigious so-
ever the variety of animals may be, yet have they
always continued from age to age perfectly regular
in their way of life, every species its own way.
We may here take notice only of the way in which
birds build their nests. How great a variety is
there in their building, yet do all those of a species build in one way. They all build in a place
which appears free from danger or disturbance,
where they may quickly bring forth and safely rear
their young. In this last both the parents commonly join but in some cases where the care of one of
them is sufficient the other leaves off attending
to them, and even there are some cases where the
young need no aid and there the parents leave them
to shift for themselves. Thus the caterpillar
----------.

From all this we see what an infinite number
of instincts belong to the brute creation and all
precisely suited to their manner of life with great
skill, and of this we can have no solution, but in
concluding that they were so ordered by the wisdom
of him who ruleth over all Nature. If again we consider their bodies we will find a vast variety, but
at the same time the structure of each admirably
suited to their way of life. Thus, we see that
some animals such as quadrupeds, who can easily
turn their head have their eyes placed on the side
of the head, but others who have not this power of
turning their head, have eyes all round and behind
as well as before. Some flies, and bees too have
two crusts like hemispheres on the sides of the
head, in each of which are inserted a great number
of eyes, in each of which there is a distinct picture formed, each of which have a distinct optic
nerve and thus they see in every direction. In
Spiders some have 4 eyes and some have 6. In the
Male they are all covered with hair so as to be
safe in pushing thro' the earth and are so small
as to be hardly discernible yet are sufficient to
warn them when they are above ground. And in those
animals that have occasion to push among trees and
bushes and the eye is defended with what is called
a membrana militans. In the other senses too there

33

is the same beautifull variety and wise contrivance.
One being endowed, where their situations require
it, with a wonderfull acuteness of Sight, another
of Taste and so on, by which they may distinguish
wholesome from poisonous food. For this reason,
depending on their taste when people are ship-
wrecked in warm climates and come to woods where
varieties of fruit present themselves, they think
they may safely eat these in which they see marks
of the birds beginning to feed upon, but those that
are untouched they suspect as noxious. Tis evident
that some of the animals are intended for the use
of others to serve them as prey, but still more
were intended for the use of Men. The ox was intended to assist him in his labourious employments,
the horse the dog and the Elephant were all designed for the service of Man and they have generally such instincts as fit them for this purpose.
The dog especially seems intended to be his compan-
ion. If we can trust to Golben, a traveller, there
are great numbers of dogs that run wild in troops
without a master and tho' they prey on every kind
of beast yet they never prey upon man, nay, so
great is their reverence for him that they will allow him to carry off what they have caught without
hurting him.


ENDNOTE for Lect: 76th


[5]My old (1958) edition of the Encyclopaedia
Britannica has an article on 'Botany' which refers
to the work done by Marcello Malpighi and Nehemiah
Grew between 1670 and 1674; Reid was perfectly right.

But it would be impossible to enumerate every
mark of wisdom to be met with in the animal creation for every part shews it. These I have mentioned seem to be regulated by fixt laws, they manifest certain ends to which there are proportioned
means, and must satisfy every candid mind that he
who made them is divine, and that chance never
could produce them. I shall now consider the marks
of wisdom to be met with in the Body of Man. It is
impossible not to see that man was intended to take
care of his own preservation, by food and drink and
by alternate labour and repose and we see that his
constitution is fitted for this purpose. As it is
necessary that his body should be supplied with
food, this is taken into the Mouth which we find
adopted to this end, to prepare it for digestion
in the Stomach. The mouth is furnished with the
tongue, teeth and of glands all of them admirably
contrived for their several ends. The teeth in
order to grind and comminute it, while mixing with
a fluid secreted by the glands, it is fitted to
pass thro the gullet without entering it. We see
likewise that these teeth are not perfectly formed
in infants, this would be inconvenient for the
Mothers in suckling them, they are only a pellucid
muscilage in that socket or cavity in the jawbone
which afterwards receives them and holds them so
firmly by degrees they grow into a greater consis-
tency as small opaque specks appear in the middle
and they gradually harden and push up till they
penetrate the gum. It may be remarked that all
our upper bones are covered with a covering called
the periosteum which is necessary to nourish them,

35

but the teeth have it not, but tho' they had it it
would soon be worn down and destroyed and so be of
no use. They appear of different forms and are designed for different purposes, some to cut and
others to ground the food we eat, hence they are
divided into two kinds by the Anatomists, the enci-
sores and molares, each of which we see are fitted
for the ends intended. And that man surely must
either be stupidly blind or obstinately perverse
who does not see that all the structure of the
mouth is not the most proper of any that could be
thought of, to receive our food and preparing it
for being digested. The preparations too made for
swallowing our food are admirable. Were we left
to do this by our own act we would of necessity
starve, but we see it is done without any care of
ours. The Stomach also is evidently intended for
digesting our food, being by its structure fitted
for the purpose and having certain glands in order
to offset it. We know likewise that the byle is
thrown into the Stomach and mixes with the contents
of the stomach and guts so as to help the digestion.
There are innumerable small vessels which are called
lacteal, fitted to receive what enters into them
while the rest is carried down and goes off. What
is separated by these vessels is carried by other
vessels and mixes with the blood in the left sub-
clavian vein where by means unknown to us it is
assimilated with the blood and makes that fluid
which is so necessary to our existence. The systems of the veins and arteries have also a most
wonderfull constitution. This blood being collected together by the veins, and brought to the
right auricle of the head, is, from thence conveyed by the pulmonary vein to the lungs / thro'
which many branches of that vein are spread / where
mixing with the air, it is fitted for our support,
from thence it returns to the left auricle of the
heart and from thence is thrown into a great artery.

The muscles of the heart have a strength pro-
portionate to the work they are to bear. They contract and dilate alternately with great force without any intention on our part. But as we know
from the principles of philosophy, that the blood

exits equally in all directions, we would be apt
to think that it would return back, but nature is
never deficient in any of her operations, she has
guarded against this by valves which afford an easy
passage out to the blood but hinder it effectually
from returning, so that it is still protruded fore-
ward and the arteries being constructed with valves
of a similar kind, it is thus carried to the utmost
extremities of the body. This circulation of the
blood was unknown to the antients. We owe the discovery to the famous Dr. Harvey, Physician to
Charles I, it is now universally adopted and is sufficiently evident in men and all other animals that
seem to have blood. In all we observe a fluid which
tho' not red yet supplies the place of it. The construction of the vessels thro' which this fluid cir-
culates is exquisite and wisely contrived. No hy-
draulic or Hydrostatic machine can better serve
their purposes. And as we are ready to admire any
contrivance for conveying water from one place to
another and the like, so ought we to admire the
invention of Nature in adapting the vessels of the
head, the arteries and to the circulation of the
blood. But from this common mass of blood there
arises other fluids to be secreted by the glands,
the whole mystery of which we are unable to discern. As there is a system of veins and arteries
for circulating the blood which divide into smaller
and smaller branches till they reach the farthest
extremities of the body, so Nature in case they
should be hurt by bruises or even destroyed by am-
putation perhaps, has provided against the contin-
gencies by making communications in many places between the arteries and the veins and between the
arteries themselves. The communications of an am-
putation are at first small, but they widen by degrees and the circulation goes on as freely as be-
fore--Another mark of wisdom in the structure of
the Body is the system of veins and nerves. These
we know are the instruments both of sensation and
of muscular motion tho' we know not how they perform their offices. The brain from which many of
them issue is admirably guarded by the bones of the
head which enclose it and defend it from internal
injury. These are at a small distance from each

other in infants and are capable of a small degree
of compression, but by degrees become indented in
one another and become so firm as to form a firm
covering to the brain. This is also guarded by
two coats called the dura mater and the pia mater
and from these two coats proceed films which go
along with all the other nerves that proceed from
the brain. But besides the brain there are nerves
which proceed also from the Spinal marrow. These
too are guarded by the back bone from injurys, but
as the back is often obliged to be bent, it is
formed that it may yield without hurting the marrow. From these two, the brain and spinal marrow,
do all the nerves proceed in pairs. It is commonly
thought that there are about 39 or 40 pairs of them,
for in some particular person there may be a small
difference yet in general they are similar, so that
the descriptions found in anatomical books are commonly found to answer. The nerves extend to all
parts of the body, so that a pin point cannot be
set down without touching some of them and they are
so distributed because they are the instruments of
sensation, so that if a nerve is cut it has no more
feeling than if it were not a part of the body.
They are then divided into smaller and smaller
branches till they become imperceptible to the
sight. How they perform their office Anatomists
and Physiologists never have been able to discover.
They do not appear to have any fluid in them like
the veins, they are rather solid, tho' of a soft
and medullary substance. But tho' we know not the
manner how they perform their office, yet by the
effects we see, that they are fitted for it. From
the nerves the power is conveyed to the muscles,
by which they contract and dilate and so produce
all the motions of the body. The muscles are of a
fleshy substance, being more so in the middle and
a kind of tendons round it by which they are drawn
together and perform their motions. The famous
Borelli, an Italian Philosopher, calculated the
strength necessary on our muscular exertions.
Their strength indeed must be prodigiously great,
because by a Law of Mechanics, the nearer a force
is to the fulcrum or centre of motion the greater
must it be, and for the conveniency of the Body,

and to prevent it from being too bulky, the force
exerted by the muscle must be very near the centre
of motion. The muscles of the arm for instance
must be within an inch and a half of their centre
of motion and yet the force to be moved may be two
feet distance, so that the strength of the muscle
must be the force as two feet is to an inch to an
inch and a half. In this Borelli calculated the
force necessary for all the muscle and we see that
Nature has adapted them exactly to it. They are
not insufficient for the force they require for
there are no instances of them being broke. They
have been shewn by anatomists to be admirably fitted for giving motion to the body. How they are
contrived is beyond our comprehension, but when a
muscle acts we know that it swells in breadth and
contracts in length and thus the motion is produced.
We know that this power is communicated to them by
the nerves, but of the manner of its operation we
are entirely ignorant--so far is the wisdom of God
beyond the wisdom of Man. That these muscles may
move easily without injuring themselves or one
another, they are all surrounded with a membrane
which is commonly moistened with fat, that at once
lubricates them, but also fills up all the inter-
stices so as to add beauty to the whole. When this
is taken away, and the muscle made bare the Body
appears a most horrid spectacle--we may observe
that the whole body in order to be preserved in its
curious organization, must have one common cover,
and here Nature has also shewn her wisdom and design in making a skin, which is a tough membrane
capable of great contraction and dilation, so that
whether a person is fat or lean, young or old, it
affords a close cover. This skin is preserved by
a cuticula or scarf skin and as this is much ex-
posed to injuries it is renewed when rubbed off.
It consists of scales which are easily perceived
by a microscope. It is this cuticula that is
raised by a blistering plaister, and we then see
how tender the real skin and how impossible it
would be to live without this. But we must not
omit that besides the nerves that are for the muscular motions there are others for the various
senses, one pair called the optical which are the

instruments of Seeing, another called the [olfacto-
ry][6] which is the instrument of Smelling, the auditory for hearing, and other small fibres of nerves
which go to the various parts of the body and are
the instruments of touch. These however are collected in greater number in the greatest number at
the points of the fingers. We are at as great a
loss to say how these nerves perform their functions
as those that are intended for the muscles. We see
no difference in their construction, and yet we see
that one kind are fitted for giving sensation and
perception, and the other only for giving motion.
There are holes in the skull I opine exactly fitted
for the transmission of the nerves to all parts of
the Body. The optic nerves enter the bottom of the
orbit of the Eyes and is fixed in the globe of the
Eye, where if it is cut or obstructed there is no
distinct vision, tho' the eye be perfectly sound.
The same happens of all the other nerves, tho' we
are ignorant what impulse is necessary towards their
communicating sensation and Perception to the Mind.
Besides the nerves for sensation, there are also
external organs of admirable contrivance. The Eye
is an organ admirably fitted for Vision. It is necessary that a picture of the object should be formed
on the coat called the Lunica(?) Retina. How this
conveys the image to the brain anatomists know not,
but this they know that when the image is not properly formed the vision is hurt or destroyed. It
would be difficult perhaps to make those who don't
understand anatomy, comprehend all that is known
of this little organ. I shall not therefore enter
on the task but those who have the least discern-
ment will observe that it is intended for seeing
and therefore that the rays of light are fitted for
it and it for them, with admirable skill. Nothing
can be more surprising than that by a small ball
fixed in a socket we can perceive the fixed stars
and the various objects around'us by means of the
refraction of the rays of light. These rays move
with such rapidity as are adapted to this end. The
other organs of sense contain no less marks of wisdom, tho' we are more at a loss with regard to the
use of their several parts. The external ear is
well fitted to receive the undulations of the

external air that produces Sound. These are conveyed to the <u>Membrana Timpanea</u>. In the inside there are several small bones that receive the impression made by the motion of it, and so it is conveyed to the auditory nerve which is spread over the inner ear. The nerve for smell is also spread over the internal part of the Nose and the nerves intended for smell are diffused over the tongue, palate, and circumambient parts. Every part there is fitted for its proper use. If therefore upon seeing a curious engine we conceive that it had a wise and skillfull Maker, must we not in a much higher degree apply these qualities to [the] contriver and maker of the curious fabric of the human body. This argument is elegantly summed up by the Sacred Writer. He that made the Eye, shall he not see? He that made the ear shall he not hear? He that gave a man understanding shall he not understand? No argument can be more forcible to any candid and ingenious mind. I might also take notice of the structure of the bones, these supports of the human body, so admirably constructed for use. While the body is in the foetus the bones are soft and flexible without any of that strength and solidity which they afterwards acquire, but as they are intended for supports, they gradually acquire a firmness of texture which is in no other part of the body. They have various articulations, some of resembling a ball and a socket, fit for turning in all directions as, for instance, those that join the arm to the shoulder and the thigh bone to the <u>os Sacrum</u>. Of the other <u>joints</u> there are different forms, all suited to their ends, and by all of these joined together we are fitted for walking, running, jumping, stooping and the like, which we do with great ease and facility. Besides these articulations for motion, there are other parts <u>not</u> intended to be removed, where the bones are not jointed, but firmly joined to one another, in a manner something like what the Carpenters call <u>dove-tailing</u>. This is the case with the two parts of the Skull. In some articulations the motions are intended to be small, such as the back's and are accordingly the bones of it are fitted so as to move a very little. In some cases again we see that motion is performed merely by the bones being joined by a cartilage or intermediate substance between bones and flesh. In this manner are the ribs joined to the breast bone. We may observe too that all the bones which touch one another are smooth and lubricous at the ends so as to make their motion more easy, all of their structure exactly answering to the laws of Motion. It is worth noticing before we conclude that the famous philosopher and Physician Galileo, having been brought up on the Epicurean tenets of a fortuitous concourse of atoms and that there was no providence, no case of a Deity, when he had occasion to consider the Structure of the human Body, was soon converted from his principles and convinced of the existence of a wise and designing Being.


ENDNOTE for Lect. 77th


[6]There is a word omitted, probably 'olfactory'.

Lect. 78<sup>th</sup>

To what I have already said I may now add that
provision which Nature had made for the cure of diseases. As we are liable to many accidents which are
apt to produce disorders in our bodies. The wisdom
of Nature hath likewise provided for the cure of
these. When any of our bones are broken there is a
fluid which issues out, at first it is of a cartilag-
inous nature, by degrees however it hardens and becomes as firm as before. All that is done by the
Physician is not to disturb nature in her operations.
It is the same with the cure of our other diseases.
It is the operation, not of Medicine, all that does
is to exclude the action of the air or whatever may
prevent nature in her processes. This seems to have
been the conception which Hippocrates and the antients had of Medicine, that it only was usefull in
aiding Nature without pretending to assume to merit
to itself. We see too when extraneous bodies are
anyhow admitted into the body, they are frequently
expelled in a very wonderfull manner. Of this
there are innumerable instances in the history of
Medicine. But I now proceed to the last branch of
this division, viz., the marks of intelligence and
wisdom to be found in the structure of the Human
Mind.

In the structure of the human Mind we may perceive various intentions and at the same time observe means fitted to answer those intentions. And

1. It is evident that man was intended to take
care of his own preservation, to avoid those hurts
that would impair his health or endanger his life,

43

and also that he should seek what is necessary to support his life. For this purpose the infant is provided with various instincts to take care of its life. It sucks when it is hungry and swallows its food, which by art it could not learn to do, it is by the instruction of Nature. When it ails too it cries by instinct, and these cries are understood by the Mother as those around, and their bowels are moved to give it all the assistance in their power. Nature has taken care that all our desires should be attended with acute pain which lead us to see and remedy them. As food and drink are necessary to supply the waste of the body, so the appetites of hunger and thirst are given us to fulfill this end, to admonish us when they should be gratified, and without these we could not know when, what, how much, or how often to eat or drink. As alternate labour and alternate rest are necessary to our health and even to our life, so nature has given us a disposition to alternate exercise and repose, by admonishing us when we have continued too long in either. The love of life and an aversion to whatever has a tendency to destroy it is implanted in all animals, in order to induce them to take care of their life, and so we find that there is no animal but what uses all the means in its power to preserve or prolong its life.

2. Another instance of wisdom in the structure of the Mind is an intention that the race should be continued. This we see, too, in the other animals as well as Man and they are all accordingly fitted with appetites to answer that end. In the human race the love of the sexes and the parental affection serves the end. In all ages whether men are wise or foolish, virtuous or vitious we can see no reason why the race should ever cease. In all situations Nature has provided against this and indeed if it were otherwise the race must very soon perish as individuals are only shortlived and temporary beings. For this purpose too Nature hath furnished the Mother with Milk and has taught the infant by instinct to suck it. Whether we consider the weaknesses or the wants of children it is evidently impossible that they could support themselves

44

without the tender care of the parents, particularly of the Mother who often deprives herself of rest and all the conveniences of life to supply its wants. And this takes place not only among wise and enlightened nations, they might perhaps do it from a principle of duty, but it takes place among all kinds of men. The different dispositions of the sexes, too, seems to have designed them for family society. This has been taken notice of in very antient times. Thus in the Economics of Xenophon we find Socrates display this very elegantly and aggreably. Nature has given the female sex that timidity and delicacy that is proper for the management of domestic affairs and the rearing of the tender offspring; to the other sex, that fortitude and courage necessary to procure subsistence for the family and which requires greater labour and robustness.

3. Nature evidently intended Man for Society, Solitude and seclusion appear unnatural and contrary to the constitution of his Nature. We see that all men in all ages have lived in this way, if we except a few individuals who either from affectation of singularity, or a wish to be thought remarkable for sanctity, or perhaps from false notions of Religion, have lived by themselves. But the intention is that we should live in Society and this intention is to be seen not in man only but in some of the lower animals, some of them we observe are gregarious, others are solitary. Foxes, lions, bears and c$^7$ associate only during the time that is requisite for copulation and the rearing of their young, black cattle and c$^7$ on the other hand are naturally gregarious and are always found in Society. Now man is evidently of the last kind, he is a gregarious animal. In all ages the principles of his Nature have led them to this state. Even the most rude and barbarous are always found in tribes or clans. Accordingly we see that he is fitted for this situation.

1. By Language which is peculiar to man. For tho' there are some signs by which the lower animals can communicate their feelings in some degree, thus, a dog can easily by his appearance warn another whether he approaches him with a friendly or a

45

hostile design, yet these signs are few, they are all natural signs understood from their nature and it is not in their power to enlarge them. But man besides the use of natural signs, is able by them to form other artificial signs and by these communicate to others not his present feelings only but his past knowledge. And thus by receiving the experience and knowledge of others to assist his own, men are perpetually improving in civility and usefull Sciences. And this seems to be peculiar to man only for it is not to be found among the brutes, they never improve--they are the same now as in former times and will remain the same to the end of the World. By language then it appears that we are intended for Society and could have no existence without it.

(2.) Men are led by natural instinct to imitate the actions of those around them. Now this has an evident relation to Society. For did we not live in Society we would have none to imitate. I might here to take notice of the social affections of which there could be no exercise without society, such as gratitude for favours received, compassion at the distresses of others, ambition of superiority and power, friendship, esteem, and benevolence, all of which serve as as many ties to bind men together in social union. Nay, even those affections which we call malevolent show that we were intended for Society as without it we could have no occasion to exercise them.

4. Nature intended man to improve in Knowledge and the usefull arts. (1) We see that he is fitted for this by his very constitution. We observe in children a great curiosity to enlarge their knowledge, they pry into whatever is unknown, everything that is new delights them, they examine it on every side and are thus daily acquiring new ideas. Children are led to this by instinct and indeed if it were not this they never would acquire any knowledge at all. (2) What tends to our improvement in knowledge and the arts is, that credulity evident to children, by which we receive with implicit submission whatever is taught them. One would be apt to think at

first sight, that we ought only to believe what we
see just reason to believe when we have sufficient
arguments to induce our belief. But were this the
case with children the consequence would be that
they would lose much of what tends to improve their
faculties and enlarge their knowledge. One of the
most remarkable parts of our constitution is the
power of acquiring habits, by which, by doing a
thing frequently we acquire a facility of doing it.
This is a power so familiar to us that we require
no account of it, but if we attend to it we will
find it altogether unaccountable, tho' we see the
ends for which it is intended. Inanimate machines
by going in a road frequently never learn to move
more easily in their road, but man is so made, that
what at first was difficult by repetition becomes
easy. By this much time is spared for our acquiring
other habits and arts. If children by repetition
did not acquire a facility of doing then they would
never walk tolerably or speak properly all their
days. The same may be said of all the other arts,
of writing, dancing, fencing and c. Habit is the
foundation of them all ----------.

Further--man was intended to improve in his
social affections. For this purpose Nature has
amixed a pleasant sensation to the exercising them.
There is a tranquility attending them which is the
comfort of life and invites us to the practice of
them as our highest happiness. On the other hand
to our malevolent affections there is an unease
mixed which admonishes us against the indulgence
of them except where they are absolutely necessary.

Further--Nature has intended us for political
Society. Tho' there be some very savage tribes
which give small marks of this, yet it is manifest
that we were designed for this. For some submission and subordination is necessary in order both
to defend us against injurys we might receive from
those of our own community or of a different one.
Even in the rudest savages as in the Canadian tribes
we find that tho' they have neither fixed laws nor
magistrates, yet it is always understood, that when
an injury to any of them by one of the same tribe

then he is entitled to revenge the quarrel, and if
from any of another tribe, then the whole tribe
think themselves bound to assist him in procuring
retaliation. And when they go a hunting or to war
there is always a kind of subordination, which tho'
rude, yet is sufficient for them. But as men improve in politeness their wants increase as stricter
union becomes necessary. The indications of Nature
which show that we were intended for this state are
① We see that men are endowed with various and
different talents. Hence, we see that all are not
equally fitted for every profession. This difference is not to be observed in the other animals.
We see a greater difference between one man and another than between any two of them. As in a building we see stones of various figures and fit for
different ends, some for cornerstones, some for
lintels, some for windows and so on so in society
we see persons are endowed with different talents
and are fitted for different offices in that Society.
And if they are endowed with these, Nature surely
intended that they should have an opportunity to
exercise them. If all lived separately and in solitude, then all would have the same things to do, so
that the same abilities would be required in all,
whereas in Society the deficiencies of one are supplied by another and all find a profession to suit
his talents--Besides ②--In large societies we find
that there are few who have either the wish or the
talents to govern. The many are tame and easily led
by a superior address. If all had the same ambition
for power and preemenence then it would be impossible that Societies should subsist. This rivalship
would effectually hinder it. But if we see that the
greatest part are easily made obedient to an ambi-
tious few, then from this we may collect that nature
intended them for government and political society.

The Last intention of Nature which I shall mention is, that men were designed to have the means
of improvement in Virtue and moral goodness. That
we have temptation to do wrong is no doubt true.
It does not appear to have been the intention of
Nature that we should be free from temptation.
This is a state of probation--but still we have

48

sufficient inducement to improve in virtue. For this end everyman is endowed with natural Conscience, which points out to him in most cases what is right and what is wrong. Self approbation follows the performance of virtuous actions, but no man can perform any crimes of an atrocious nature without remorse. Every man sees that wisdom, prudence, justice, temperance and fortitude tend to real happiness, and if at any time he yields to the force of temptation and acts contrary to the directions of Conscience, he always finds remorse follows it more than sufficient to counterbalance all the pleasure he felt in deviating from his duty. Everyone then has the means of improvement, tho' some perhaps from various circumstances, as, good education good example, he may have it in a higher degree than others--From all this it is clear, that in the structure of the human mind there appear various intentions and there are we have seen means fitted to answer these intentions, which shews wisdom and skill in the contrivance of our Constitution ----------.

Having now at some length pointed out these marks of wisdom and design which appear in various parts of the universe and shewed thus, that they arose from wise contrivance next I come to consider the account which the atheists give of the origin of all things and examine its probability in comparison of what has been already advanced.

/

ENDNOTE for Lect. 78th

[7]Archaic, apparently means "etc.".

49

Lect. 79th__

Before I proceed directly to the subject proposed in the conclusion of my last lecture it may
be proper to make some remarks with regard to the
argument which I last insisted on, viz. that from
the marks of wisdom and design to be met with in
the Universe we infer it is the work of a wise and
intelligent cause. It is worthy of notice, that
intelligence, wisdom and skill are not objects of
our external senses, nor indeed objects of consciousness in any person but ourselves, and it may
be observed, that even in ourselves we are properly
speaking [not] conscious of any either natural or
acquired habit which we possess. We are conscious
only of their effects when they are exerted. A
man's wisdom can be known only by its effects, by
the signs of it in his conduct--his eloquence by
the signs of it in his discourse. In this same
manner we judge of his courage and strength of Mind
and of all his other Virtues--it is only by their
effects that we can discern these qualities of his
Mind. Yet it may be observed that we judge of
these talents with as little hesitation as if they
were objects of our senses. One we pronounce to
be a perfect idiot incapable of doing any thing
that will be valid in law--another to have understanding and to be accountable for his actions--
one we pronounce to be open, another cunning--one
ignorant, another knowing. Every man of common
understanding forms such judgements of those he
converses with, he can no more avoid it, than he
can seeing objects that are placed before his eyes.
Yet in all these the talent is not immediately perceived, it is discerned only by the effects it

51

produces. From this it is evident that it is no
less a part of the human constitution to judge of
powers by their effects than of corporeal objects
by the senses. We see that such judgements are
common to all men and absolutely necessary in the
affairs of life, now every judgement of this kind
is only an application of that general rule, that
from marks of intelligence and wisdom in effects,
a wise and intelligent cause may be inferred.
From the wise conduct, we infer wisdom in the
cause, and from a brave conduct, we infer bravery
--this we do with perfect security--it is done by
all--they cannot avoid it, it is necessary too in
the conduct of life, it is therefore to be received
as a first principle. Some however have thought
that we learn this by reasoning or by experience.
I apprehend it can be got from neither of these.
We may observe that philosophers who can reason
excellently on subjects that admit of reason, upon
this subject appeal only to the Common sense of
Mankind, and in some cases offer instances to make
the absurdity of the opposite glaring and sometimes
using the weapons of wit and raillery which in
cases of this kind is very proper and often suc-
cessfull, Cicero in his tract De Natura Deorum,
speaks thus--Can anything done by chance have all
the marks of design? If a man throws dies and both
turn up aces, if he should throw 400 times would
chance throw up 400 aces? Colours thrown carelessly upon a canvas may have come up to appearance of
a human fact, but would they form a picture beautifull as the Pagan Venus? A Hog grubbing the Earth
with his snout may turn up something like the let-
ter A, but would he turn up the words of a complete
sentence? Thus in order to shew the absurdity of
supposing what has the marks of design could arise
from chance, he gives a variety of examples where
the absurdity is palpable without reasoning on the
matter. And we find other authors arguing in the
same way. The ingenius Mr. Hutchinson, endeavors
to prove it by reasoning and he is the only author
I have met with who has made the attempt. Without
pretending to say whether the reasoning is just or
not I shall only observe, that he has drawn arguments from chances to shew that a regular arrangement

of parts must proceed from designs, that they could not proceed from chances. It may be remarked, that this doctrine of chances as a branch of Mathematics is not yet a hundred years old, but the truth of this principle has gained the assent of all since the beginning of the world and could therefore receive little strength from that reasoning. Let us next consider whether it may not arise from experience, that from marks of design in effects we ascribe them to a designing cause. That this truth is not derived from experience is evident for two reasons. (1) Because this is a necessary truth and no Experience can discover a truth to be necessary. Thus, tho' it is consistent with our experience that twice three makes six, and the Sun always rises in the East and sets in the West, yet between these two all must perceive this distinction, that the first is a necessary truth and has been and will continue true independent of our experience or of any cause, but the latter is not a necessary truth, it is contingent and depends on the will of the Maker of the World. If two things appear to us constantly conjoined and if our experience of them is uniform, this still gives no reason to consider that they are necessarily connected or that they cannot be disjoined. In a word, Experience informs us only of what has been been, not of what shall be. Further--Experience may shew us a constant Conjunction between two things in those cases where both cases are perceived, but if one only is perceived experience never can shew it constantly conjoined with the other. For example, thought is connected with the thinking principle, but how do we know that thought may not exist without a Mind. These no doubt we find connected but if a man says he knows it by experience he deceives himself. Mind is not an object of Consciousness however-- one only of them is perceived; we can't say then that they are constantly conjoined. We conclude therefore that the necessary connection of thought and the thinking principle is not learned by Experience. The same reason applies to the inference of design in cause and effect from marks of it. The one is an object of Consciousness but not the other. Experience then cannot shew a necessary connection.

Thus it appears then that from marks of design and wisdom to infer intelligence in the cause is a first principle learned neither by reasoning nor by experience, it is self evident and assented to by all men. It is on this principle then, that my argument is grounded. There are clear marks of wisdom and design in the formation and government of the world, must they not arise then from a designing cause? And this argument has this peculiar advantage that it gathers additional strength with every improvement in knowledge, every discovery in Philosophy. We are told of Alphonzo, a Moorish king, that when his philosophers explained to him their notions of our planetary system, he said, "that he could have made a better one himself." But the system they gave him was not the work of God it was the fiction of Men, but since the present new theory was introduced no one has presumed to shew it could be better. Indeed when we attend to the marks of wisdom and intelligence that appear all around, every discovery proves a new hymn of praise to him who is the Creator and Governor of the world.

This argument has commonly been called the argument from final causes and we shall accordingly use it without enquiring into the propriety of it. If reduced to the form of a Syllogism there are the two premises. ① that an intelligent first cause may be inferred from marks of wisdom in the effects. ② There are clear marks of wisdom and design on the works of Nature--The conclusion is then--the works of Nature are effects of a designing and wise cause. Now it is evident that we must either deny the premises or admit the conclusion. The second of them I have endeavored already at some length to prove and I have also shewed that the first is got neither by reasoning nor by all men. But we find that among the Antients, that the first of them was admitted, that the things which bear the marks of wisdom and design could proceed only from an intelligent cause and not from chance, but they denied that any evidence of these were to be seen in the constitution of things. We may learn this from what we find put into the mouth of one of that atheistical sect in the 3 lib. of Cicero's De Natura

54

Deorum. But modern improvements in philosophy have shewn the folly and weakness of this assertion and none now have the affrontery to deny that clear marks of wisdom are to be seen in the works of Creation. This appeared evident to the famous Galen, who wrote a Book _____ 8, tho' he was educated an Epicurean purposely to shew that all could not proceed from chance. Those in modern times have seen the weakness of this and have that strong hold as untenable, but they have assaulted the other of the premises I mentioned, viz., that we can infer design and wisdom in the cause from discovering it in the effects. In his dispute against this principle, des Cartes, tho' he surely was not an atheist, had led the way and his motive for it probably was this, that having invented some new arguments himself for the existence of the Deity, he wishes to disparage all others in order to bring the greater credit to his own, or because he was offended perhaps with the Peripatetics for mixing final causes in their solution of the phenomena of Nature. A Physical cause is different from a final cause. The physical cause hunts out the laws of Nature from which the phenomena flow, thus, for example, we can shew that the physical cause of water rising in a pump is the weight of the atmosphere, but the final cause again hunts out the end which Nature had in view. Thus, the end of the eye is for seeing, the feet for walking and so on. These final causes des Cartes thought he could not know, he thought the philosopher had nothing to do with them, and to attempt to explain them he considered as presumptious and arrogant. In this track he was not followed by many who admired him greatly in other things, particularly by the pious Dr. Henry More of Cambridge and Fenelon, Bishop of Cambray, who has wrote a book on the existence of God and his arguments are mostly drawn from the art of Nature, as he calls it, or those tokens of wisdom and design which appear in all parts of Nature. Since the time of des Cartes however we find that some have adopted his sentiments who may be suspected of a tendency to Atheism of these we may reckon Maupertuis and Buffon but the most direct [attack, assault] against this principle has been made by Mr.

55

Hume, who puts an argument against it in the mouth
of an Epicurean on which he seems to lay great
stress--it is this--that the production of the Universe is a singular effect, to which there is no
similar instance, therefore we can draw no conclusion from it, whether it is made by wisdom and intelligence or without. I shall consider a little
the form of this objection. The amount of it is
this, that if we were accustomed to see worlds produced some by wisdom and others without it and saw
always such worlds as ours produced by a wise cause,
the conclusion would then be this world of ours was
made by wise contrivance, but as we have no experience of this kind therefore we can conclude nothing
about the matter. This conclusion of his is built
on this supposition of past experience finding two
things constantly united. But this I shewed to be
a mistake. No man ever saw wisdom, and if he does
not conclude from the marks of it, he can form no
conclusions respecting anything of his fellow creatures. How should I know that any of this audience
have understanding? It is only by the effects of
it on their conduct and behavior, and this leads me
to suppose that such behavior proceeds only from
understanding. But says Hume, unless you know it
by experience you know nothing of it. If this is
the case I never could know it at all. Hence it
appears that whoever maintains that there is no
force in the argument from final causes, denies the
existence of any intelligent being but himself. He
has the same evidence for wisdom and intelligence
in God as in a Father, or Brother or a friend. He
infers it in both from its effects and these effects
he discovers in the one as well as the other.

Having thus vindicated the argument from any
exceptions that have been brought against it I now
proceed as I proposed to consider a little the
causes which atheists assign for the Universe and
the production of all this beautifull system.

Some of them attributed it to Chance as the
antient Epicureans did, but we may observe that
chance cannot be the cause of anything and when
we say a thing happens by chance, it is a word

expressive only of our own ignorance of the cause--
chance can never be the efficient cause of any thing.
When a man throws a dice we say it is a chance which
side turns up--now, what is the meaning of this?
Chance can never be a cause, it means only that we
are unable to discover the cause, for no man can
measure the force with which he throws a dice with
such accuracy as to tell what side will turn up, and
it is so whenever we attribute to chance. When a
1000 tickets are put into a box and mixed and turned
over by the motion of the lottery wheel, a boy puts
in his hand and we say it is a chance whether he
pulls out a prize or a blank--what is the meaning
of this? It is, that no man knows what it will be
whether the one or the other, but there is no part
of it but has its cause. To assign chance then as
a cause of anything is absurd and when the atheist
tells you the Universe was produced by chance, he
means only that it was produced he does not know
how. This however does not hinder it from being
owing to some cause and that cause we have already
shewed is eternal. Besides--nothing we ascribe to
chance is regular. If a man, says Tillotson, throws
down a heap of types on the ground it is a chance
how they fall, but chance could not form them into
a poem like the Iliad or the Aenied, or even into
a discourse in Prose. Some again have attributed
all things to Necessity. But if we attend to the
meaning of the words we will see Necessity cannot
be the cause of any thing. When we speak vaguely
of causes indeed we say some of them are necessary
--others Voluntary, tho' a cause in the philosophical sense of the word signifies only an agent by
his own will producing the effect, yet in vulgar
language we apply it to any instruments or means
used to the production of the effect. So we say
the pressure of the air is the cause of the Mercury
rising in the Barometer and the necessary cause of
this is the weight of the air which is as necessary
as the effect it produces and this is produced by
its gravitation, which also must have a cause and
thus may we go on till we rise to the first cause
of all. A necessary cause then is an effect produced by another cause till we are landed in a
first cause of all which is not necessary but a

real efficient cause. We shewed before the absurdity of supposing an infinite series of causes. I
shall not now resume what was then said - - - - - - - - - .

Another refers the Universe to Nature. They
tell you Nature does so and so and that it produced
all things. A late French philosopher has wrote a
treatise in support of this doctrine, entitled Sys-
teme de la Nature[9] in which he ascribes everything
to Nature. But what does he mean by Nature?--it is
a phrase as inappropriate as chosen or Necessary.
It is common indeed to say a thing is done by Nature to distinguish it from what is done by Art.
Thus we say a Cabinet is the work of Art not of Na-
ture--a tree again is the work of Nature not of
Art. In this way we are accustomed to consider Nature as something opposite to art--we consider it
as producing something and art others. But here by
Nature we must mean it is as this produced by the
laws of Nature or by the author of Nature. Here
the phrase is intelligible, but as an efficient
cause it has no meaning. A law of Nature never
could produce anything without an intelligent being
to put them in execution. As in civil law it is
not the law which tries a man, but the judge acting
according to those laws and executing them. So the
rules of grammar never would produce a finished
creation of themselves without some one to form the
sentences according to them. In like manner a law
of Nature supposes a Lawgiver, a being who established & operates according to them. We see then
it is vain to have recourse to this Subterfuge to
say that all was produced by Nature--the term is
as unmeaning as if we said it was produced by
Chance or Necessity.

Having now insisted so long on this argument
I think it needless to insist at any length upon
others. Some have argued the matter from the unan-
imous consent of all men in all ages except those
who are so much in barbarity as hardly to merit the
name of human creatures, and also--from this--that
every part of the Creation bears marks of a recent
formation. These and several others you will find
in authors who have handled the subject, but tho'

I would be very far from disparaging those arguments
as useless, yet I would despair of convincing a man
by these who resists the force of this--such a man
is hardened beyond the power of arguments. -------
I now proceed to consider the Nature and attributes
of the Deity.


ENDNOTES for Lect. 79th


[8] I simply cannot make out this title. It appears to be Latin, probably based on earlier Greek.
I can make out just enough to be sure that this is
the work recently (1968) translated for the Cornell
University Press as On the Usefulness of Parts of
the Body.

[9] Somewhat muddled, but apparently this is the
Baron Paul Heinrich Dietrich d'Holbach (1723-1789),
whose System de la Nature appeared pseudonymously
in 1770.

This is a subject too high to be grasped by
our weak and limited capacities. When we consider
attentively the works of Nature we see clear indications of power, wisdom, and goodness, yet we see
still much remain into which we cannot penetrate
and of which we must be forever ignorant. If this
is true then in this case, may it not be expected
that our notions of the great author of all will
be imperfect and inadequate as our notions of his
works. The divine Nature indeed is a more proper
object for the humble veneration of the pious heart
than of curious disquisition to the most elevated
Understanding. The pride of philosophy however has
spurred on some to excogitate how the World might
have been created and how governed. It was from
this intemperate desire of comprehending the laws
of the Universe, that many among the antients ex-
cogitated or invented their Theogonie's or Cosmogonies, and among the moderns too gave rise to
those Theories of the Earth and of the Universal
Government of things which appear indeed rather as
the reveries of fancifull men than as truth. And
I may venture to affirm that all these Theogonies
and Cosmogonies which are not legitimately deduced
from observation will always appear as unlike the
works of God, as the castles built by children,
which the next moment they toss over with their
foot, to the most regular and finished piece of
architecture and we have reason therefore to think
that our notions of the attributes of deity will
be as imperfect as the notions we can form of his
works. This consideration then ought to make us
diffident in the conceptions we form of the Divine

Nature--we have no means of forming conceptions in
any degree adequate to the object--the Supreme Being operates, before us and behind us, on our right
hand and on our left, and even within us, but we
see him not. In rude ages, we see men generally
ascribe to him a form like that of their own with
organs and appetites similar to their own. When
men improve in refinement and knowledge, a little
reflection leads them to form new ideas of deity
as of a more spiritual nature. But tho' they do
not ascribe to him a bodily figure, or the organs
appropriate to a human Body, yet they find themselves under a necessity of assigning to him something analogous to the Human Mind, such as, understanding, will, and moral character. All our original notions of Mind and its attributes are got by
a consciousness of its operations in ourselves and
so we can form no conception of any attribute in
the Supreme Being to which there is not something
analogous in ourselves. As a blind man can form
no consciousness of Colors, or a deaf man of Sounds,
so neither can we form a notion of any thing belonging to the divine mind of which we have no consciousness in our own. And perhaps there may be
attributes belonging to the divine Nature of which
we can form no more a conception than a blind man
has of colors. It may be proper then, to point out
the topics from which we commonly reason on this
subject before we proceed to consider particularly
his Nature and attributes and these I think may be
reduced to three heads. 1. From the appearance of
such attributes in the operations of Nature we may
collect that they exist in the Deity. Thus, from
the appearance of wisdom in the structure of things
we may collect his wisdom and from the tokens or
appearances of good contrivance--of such contrivance as tends to the good and happiness of his
creature--we may collect his goodness. This is
precisely like collecting the characters of Men
from their ordinary conduct and it is indeed the
chief source from which by reason we collect the
attributes of the divine Nature--from the tenor of
his conduct in the administration of things as far
as they fall under our view. 2. We may reason
with regard to some of the divine attributes, from

his necessary existence. As it is evident that this is an attribute belonging to the deity, so it lays a foundation for our reasoning to some of his other attributes. This is a mode of existence quite different from that of those beings that are merely contingent and perhaps draws consequences with it which by no means result from it. 3. In like manner we argue from his unlimited perfections. If it appears that we should ascribe to deity every perfection in the highest degree, we may from hence deduce more accurate notions of some of his attributes. These I think are the different topics from which authors have reasoned with regard to the attributes of deity, notwithstanding some have advanced it as a fixt point that we can reason only from the first of these topics, viz. from the appearance of his attributes in the operation of Nature we may collect that they exist in him. This Mr. Hume lays down as a first principle and thence draws it as a consequence, that we ought to ascribe to the Deity no higher degree of wisdom and goodness than what appears in the construction of his works and from this he endeavors to conclude that we ought to ascribe to him not these qualities in an unlimited degree, but only in a certain inferred limited proportion. The argument is grounded on this, it is to be observed that we can reason with respect to the Nature and attributes of Deity from no other topic but from the appearances of these attributes in the contrivance and governance of things.

Having premised these things I may remark that the attributes of the Supreme Being are commonly distinguished into two classes, his natural and-- his moral attributes. I shall begin with the first. By natural attributes we understand those in which his will is not concerned. By the moral attributes those which give direction to his will and conduct. Of the Natural attributes of deity the first we take notice of is his

Eternity--that is his being without beginning or end of existence or as the Sacred writer prettily expresses it, "from everlasting to everlasting God." Our notions of his eternity are derived from the

notions we form of duration. We have an immediate
and instinctive belief of duration in every act of
Memory. For it is essential to this that it relate
to something past and that some interval of duration
has interposed between it and the present. Every
man in every act of remembrance has a conception of
duration but there is something peculiar in this
conception of duration, that, tho' we can assign
limits to our own duration--to the duration of
every created being yet we can assign none to duration itself. We had a beginning, but duration did
not begin with us. There was a time when we were
not, but then duration was. So it is with every
being created by God--put their beginning as far
back as you please, still if they had a beginning,
there must have been a time when they were not and
therefore duration did not begin with it. We see
then tho' the whole creation had a beginning yet
Duration could have none. Its nature will not permit us to believe that it had a beginning and neither can it have any end. We see no impossibility
in supposing all created things annihilated in a
moment and others created in their stead, but this
would be impossible if duration did not continue to
flow equally when no created being existed. Thus
we see that Duration considered in itself is neces-
sary--it had no beginning and will have no end and
we cannot suppose it limited without contradiction.
Things which have a beginning occupy only a small
past which bear no more proportion to duration than
finite to infinity. If we consider a straight line
drawn out without beginning or end, any part of it
that could be measured, by inches or feet or even
miles would bear no proportion to the whole. Such
a part must have a beginning and an end. It can
have no proportion then or as arithmeticians say
it cannot be an aliquot part of the whole which has
neither beginning nor end.

    . Another thing remarkable in the Nature of Du-
ration is, that as it is unlimited so it is necessarily existing. We cannot say so of our own Selves.
For tho' we have existed for a certain time, yet
there is no absurdity in supposing that there was
a time when we did not exist or when we will not

exist. It depended on the will of God and he might
give us existence or might not give it--it is a
contingent event which may be or may not be. But
can we say so of Absolute duration?--by no means--
it involves an absurdity in supposing there was a
time in which it did not exist or will not exist--
Having premised these things with regard to Duration, I apprehend that there is no argument necessary to shew that the Deity is, was, and will be
in all points of duration. His existence is com-
mensurate with duration and there is no point of it
in which he will not exist. And perhaps after all
this conception of the deity is inadequate and puerile. It is however the only one which our limited
faculties can reach. Some of the Schoolmen thought
to form a more adequate notion of duration by calling
it "a moment continued forever without alteration"
but this definition involves an absurdity in it and
instead of throwing light on the Subject rather
darkens it; for to suppose any point of duration to
stand still involves a contradiction and it is inconsistent with every notion of duration which we
can form. It may be observed that all men even
atheists themselves, allow that something must have
been Eternal and indeed this is evident from the
first principle which I have already mentioned,
that nothing can begin to exist without a cause and
for the same reason it will follow, that what is
uncaused and not produced by the power and wisdom
of some other being must be eternal. / Against any
existence from eternity some objections have been
brought, but they conclude equally against duration
itself. The objections amount to this. That in
the infinity of duration which is past, there must
be a certain number of years, but there must 12
twelve times as many months as years and 365 times
as many days as months, which is to make one infinity 12 times or 365 times as great as another. But
if it shews anything [it] leads us [to] think duration had a beginning which is absurd. The fallacy
of the reasoning lies in this--that we apply years
and months and days to measure that which from its
very nature admits of no measure--infinity is im-
measurable. Sometimes we apply infinite to express
any large indeterminate number. In this sense it

is intelligible and in this sense eternity may be said to contain an infinity of years, that is that no number of years can equal eternity. But if we use infinite to express any determinate number, then it is absurd and involves a contradiction no less than if we should talk of a square circle.

Another attribute of Deity--is his necessary existence, that is that it is impossible that he could not be. Every being that exists is either contingent or necessary. These two ways then opposed to each other are contradictory and therefore one or other is applicable to every being. We call that contingent which either might or might not be and that necessary which must be. Whatever either might or might not be depends on the will of some agent with power to bring it to pass or not--a power to produce evidently implies a power also not to produce--hence it follows that whatever be cause of any existence--its existence is contingent and depends on the will of the agent whether it should exist or not. That we do exist is most certain-- but that existence is contingent, the Supreme Being gave it and he can take it away when he pleases--it depends on his will. But are we to suppose that the Supreme Being himself exists in the same manner, this evidently would be absurd; he derives his power and his existence from no other being. Therefore he is not contingent but necessary. As necessary existence is a mode of existence of which no other Being but the Supreme Being is possessed, no wonder it is too big for our weak faculties and that we find it difficult to conceive it. In order to assist our Conceptions we may illustrate the distinction of Necessary and contingent Existence by the distinction between truths, which are also divided into Necessary and Contingent. Some truths we perceive manifestly to be necessary such as are all the truths of Mathematics, as this, that equals added to unequals makes the whole unequal and these we perceive are necessary, they must be true in all times and in all places without variation or change --they depend not for their truth on the will of any being. But there are truths of another kind, which are contingent, thus the Sun has always

continued to rise in the East and set in the West--
this is a truth confirmed by uniform experience,
nevertheless it is not a necessary truth--there is
no contradiction in supposing the course of the Sun
to be quite opposite to rise in the West and to set
in the East--it depends entirely on the Will of the
Supreme Being that the one course takes place and
not the other.  Thus have we seen the distinction
between Necessary and contingent truths--that the
one is true in all times and in all places and depends not on the will of any being--that on the
other hand, contingent truths depend on the Will
and power of the being who produced them.  Now
there is a similitude tho' imperfect here to necessary and contingent existence.  That is necessary
existence which cannot not be, which must be and
which depends not on the Will of any being.  That
again is contingent existence, which arose from a
cause, which depends upon that power and may cease
to be if that cause alters.  ----------

The next natural attribute of the Deity which
I shall consider is his Immensity--that is, that
he is every where present, of a thing so far above
us our conceptions must be inadequate.  A child has
only a dark and indistinct conception of those nobler powers in man which have not yet unfolded themselves in his infant heart, so our notions of the
divine perfections and attributes must always be
imperfect and puerile.  Now we see them only darkly
as thro' a glass and judge of them as children do
of matters beyond their comprehension.  We can attribute nothing to deity of which there is not some
faint ray or resemblances in ourselves.  Whatever
we perceive of real excellence in ourselves in our
own Mind which is the work of God, it must be in
the author of it.  For no reasoning can be more
convincing than this used by the Psalmist, "he that
made the ear shall he not hear?  he that made the
eye shall he not see?  he that gave man understanding shall himself not understand?"  So if he has
given man, the work of his hands a certain sphere
of action shall not he himself act in a sphere for
more extensive and circumscribed by no narrow
bounds.  We have however I apprehend a more distinct

notion how body occupies Space than how the Mind
does. By the sense of touch we receive certain notions of the places of Body, we know that two bodies
can't occupy the same place at the same time. We
know too that Body is in its Nature finite, limited,
and composed of parts totally independent of each
other, yet Space is in its Nature unlimited and indivisible. We cannot call Space a Substance--nei-
ther can we call it relation with any modification
of any substance, yet it is something of which we
have a distinct conception. The subject is dark
and intricate--there is something in the Nature of
Space which overpowers and is sufficient to humble
the most elevated Understandings when they see they
cannot comprehend its Nature. Without then making
any further reflections upon it myself I shall lay
before the sentiments of one of the most profound
and penetrating geniuses ever the World produced,
I mean Sir Isaac Newton. They are to be found in
the Scholium annexed to his <u>Principia</u>--"Deus eternus
est et infinitus, omniprecens and omniscius and
c___ cognoscinus"[10]--No human authority can be
greater than this and they are the result of that
deep reflection on the works of Nature, which makes
him the lasting honour of his age and country. His
great merit has been admirably and concisely displayed by Mr. Pope in these two lines

"Nature and Nature's Laws were hid in night;
God said, Let Newton be, and all was Light."


ENDNOTE for Lect. 80th


[10]This translates, "God is eternal and infinite,
omnipresent and all wise and c--- we know."

Lect. 81$^{st}$

We are at a loss in what sense to ascribe
place to the Mind. The Schoolmen maintain that it
was "Totus in toto & totus in omni parti".[11] But
this is so far from throwing light on the subject
that it darkens it. We rather should acknowledge
our ignorance & confess this to be one of the many
things beyond the reach of the human faculties.
They must have a manner of existing in place totally unlike to body--a certain Nature in which they
act & we cannot conceive action without an agent.
Since then we find in ourselves a limited sphere
of action & that we exist in a limited Space, it
may (be) asked what sphere of action or what place
can be ascribed to that being who is himself uncaused & the cause of all things; who is from everlasting to everlasting & who has unlimited duration
with his existence & whose existence is no less
necessary than endless duration and unlimited Space.
Shall we consider such a one as confined by any
limits? I conceive the most natural notion we can
form is agreeable to that we have been endeavoring
to establish, that unlimited Space is the sphere
of his Power & that it is filled by his Immensity
as duration is by his Eternity. But to reason
more closely--the argument which reason suggests
on this Subject are chiefly two 1. We see marks
of his wisdom & power in all the parts of the Universe which fall under one view. 2. We may infer
his Immensity from his Necessary Existence.

1. There are manifest indications of his power and presence thro' every part of his wide extended dominions. For all being was first created

69

by an act of his will & power & surely could not be
existent when the agent was not. He laid the foundation of the Earth & the heavens, nay the heaven
of heavens is the work of his hands. The most distant of the fixed stars also were made by him, nor
when we consider their distance, yet that their tho'
12,000 miles distance are made visible to us, that
they are in magnitude & lustre not inferior to our
Sun & if we judge by Analogy, who are as distant
from one as from us & each having his primaries &
secondaries revolving round him. If to this we add
the immense number we see even by the naked eye &
the still greater number by the telescopes, when,
I say, we consider the Supreme Being as exerting
his power & presence thro' this prodigious extent
of Space, what measure can we set to his being, or
to what limits of space can we suppose him confined?

Further--We are not to suppose the divine operations to cease, merely on giving existence to these
objects. We see many changes & revolutions in Nature which requires the finger of Omnipotence to
perform them, tho to us they appear regulated by
fixed laws. But we should observe, that the laws
by which a being acts is one thing, & the being who
acts agreeable to these laws is a different thing.
It requires power & authority to act agreeable to
laws, as well as to act without them. The being
who acts without them we consider as possessed of
no wisdom nor goodness, but he who acts by them we
consider as possessed of wisdom & goodness & of power nevertheless.

Now the Laws of Nature regular, constant & uniform not only display his goodness & wisdom but require also his constant operation & therefore require his presence in all parts of duration. We
formerly took notice of the Laws of Nature in the
vegetative & animal kingdom as excellent & regular
--in the manner of propagating their species, so
various in the different kinds & so uniform in the
individuals of each kind in their manner of growth
& of drawing nourishment--in the uniformity of their
structure--and in a remarkable manner we perceive
his operation in the instincts of animals & in the

70

gradual evolutions of the powers of the Human Mind.
In the animal kingdom too there are many laws of
Nature no less uniform & constant as the cohesion
of the particles of matter--their corpuscular(?)
attraction--various chemical affinities--all of affecting not only at small distances but affecting
every particle of--there are other powers, as mag-
netism--it affects indeed at a greater distance but
affects only one kind of iron matter--there are
others still more extensive than this--thus, gravitation acts not only on every particle of matter on
the surface of our Earth but to every part of the
Solar System & by it every particle in that system
acts on & is itself acted upon by every other particle. Whether this power extends to the fixed stars
we know not, but this we know that the rays of
light coming from them are subject to the same laws
of refraction & reflection with the light in our
own planets--the same laws of Nature thus operate
thro' all uniformly & regularly--

2. There is an absurdity in supposing limits
to a being, either in time or place, who exists
necessarily. For this necessity is the same at all
times & at all places & therefore we cannot suppose
a being necessarily existing in any place which is
not necessarily existing in another place. Tho'
our notion of this kind of existence, as observed
before is imperfect & inadequate, yet we can have
a clearer conception of it, by attending to the
distinction of truths into necessary & contingent,
& this is an evident property of truths which are
necessary, that they are true in all places & at
all times, & could not possibly be otherwise. We
conceive Space and Duration to exist necessarily,
& therefore conceive them unlimited from their very
Nature, & we can as easily conceive them not to
exist as not to exist always & everywhere. What
exists necessarily then exists everywhere & at all
times, having no relation to one place or one thing
which it has to another.

Another attribute we have reason to ascribe
to the deity is Unlimited Power--His power is manifested 1. In the works of creation. The power

71

exerted in Creation is beyond our conception, for our human power consists in applying causes to effects actions to things passive but cannot produce a single particle of matter not before existing, nor can we annihilate a single particle that God has made. Indeed all the operations of Nature which we see consists in various combinations, compositions & decompositions of what is already made without either creations of new or annihilations of old. But it was not so from all Eternity--matter is a thing so imperfect that to ascribe an eternity of existence to it is absurd--all must be ascribed to the Deity, the great first cause of all--

2. His power is manifested in governing the world. To suppose, with Leibnitz, that everything when created was endowed with such internal powers as to produce all the changes that afterwards happen is then to exclude all divine management together. But we have no reason to think that the world is governed in this way, without the interposition of the Supreme Being. Nature leads us to conceive the Maker of the universe as its constant governor, and leads us to apply to him as the hearer of prayer & the kind protection of his rational offspring. The weak & imperfect power of man is soon exhausted, but the power of the almighty is subject to no lassitude or fatigue. We must not include however in our notion of his omnipotence the doing things impossible. This notion we find was advanced by des Cartes on purpose to support some parts of his system. We would not say, be it that Deity could do things impossible; this is a mistake into which that philosopher would not have fallen had it not been that to support a favorite theory. For to that what is impossible is a contradiction in the Nature of things--we may as well conceive a thing to be & not to be at the same time. There are certain things which we perceive are necessarily true, now to suppose these subject to any power, even infinite power, is absurd for what is necessarily true is always true. Another thing we cannot suppose the divine power to extend to, is, his <u>moral Nature</u>. It is absurd to suppose that he has <u>the power of</u> depriving himself of any

of his perfections, as, his goodness, wisdom, justice, etc. It is no less absurd to suppose his
power to extend to his moral Nature. When talking
of a good or virtuous man, we say that it is impossible he should cheat or do an immoral thing; this
expression is perhaps too strong when applied to
Man, but it holds with respect to the Deity & is
to be considered not as an impeachment of his honor
but as an expression of his certitude--not a defect
of his Nature but a perfection of moral goodness---.

Another attribute of the deity is Unlimited
Perfection. This indeed is rather a general declaration of his attributes than of any one or ones
in particular, but it was necessary to take notice
of it as from it we may argue some other of his
perfections.

It may be observed that there are some notions
of the Mind, which are general & abstract, yet are
found in every individual of the species & that too
very early, of this kind are our notions of good &
ill, & what is nearly allied to these of perfection
& imperfection. We give the name of perfection, to
that which every good man values in himself or in
others, what he wishes not to lose, altho' men from
different degrees of moral refinement may differ in
their estimation of the value of things external,
yet we find a very great unanimity in what qualities
of this kind are properly called excellences or perfections. Thus everybody agrees, that ignorance &
folly are imperfections, that knowledge & wisdom
are perfections. All agree that power is a perfection and impotence an imperfection--that selfcommand
is a perfection & being a slave to passion or appe-
tite is an imperfection. To do what we know to be
wrong & what we will afterwards repent & be sorry
for, is an imperfection, to pursue steadily what is
proper & right is a perfection. Indeed I believe
there is nothing in which men are more generally
agreed, than in the application of these terms of
perfection & imperfection to the qualities of the
Mind. This shows us that these terms are not words
without meaning, nor do they depend for their truth
on the variable tastes of individuals, but that

73

there is some common Standard by which they may be measured. Whatever implies defect, weakness, or disappointment or misery, we call imperfection-- Whatever is the object of esteem, love, veneration or admiration we consider as a perfection. Having thus laid down our notion of perfection & imperfection what reason have we to the Supreme Being every perfection in the highest degree?

1. It ought to be considered that every perfection or real excellence which we perceive in the creation belongs to a much higher degree to the Creator & perhaps in Deity there may be perfections of which we have no more a conception than a blind man of colours. If this is true however, as undoubtedly it is, that every perfection as the effect is to be found in the cause, then we must conclude that every real excellence we discover in God's Creation are only faint rays of more eminent perfections to be found in the Creator of all. But, 2. reason teaches us not only to the Supreme Being, perfection only in a superior degree but even in the highest degree. We, his creatures are possessed only of that portion which he willed to bestow upon us--it is bounded by narrow limits. But what bounds can be set to his perfections, who is necessarily existent & who is unlimited?

Another natural attribute of Deity is Perfect Knowledge & Wisdom. The arguments reason suggests here are chiefly these two. 1. The marks of wisdom & design to be seen in the works of Creation. In all the parts of Nature, in water, air, earth & sea--in the distribution of things upon the Earth's Surface--in the wonderful variety of vegetables & the no less wonderful variety of animals-- in the structure & instincts of animals--in the structure of the human body & Mind--in all of these, we found marks of a wise artificer. The more we knew of his works, the more our admiration of his wisdom was raised. As, yon man ignorant of Clockwork, when he looks at the outside admires the regularity with which he observes the hours & minutes & seconds & can't help thinking that it required knowledge & contrivance to execute it but when he

74

is allowed to look into it & see the beauty & exquisite contrivance of the parts of the whole how will his admiration of the skill of the maker be raised? It is so with his admiration of the skill of the great artist who formed the Universe. The various parts of the vast machine excite our surprise & wonder, but we are the more struck the skill & wisdom which executed the whole. The wisdom & knowledge of others around us are discovered only by the signs of them in their conduct & actions, now we have the same evidence of the wisdom of the deity & in a much higher degree. It may be observed. 2 The Supreme Being knows all his creatures & all their qualities. As it was him who first created them & who still governs them. The artificer knows his own workmanship. 3 We have reason to ascribe knowledge & wisdom to deity because it is a perfection. I formerly endeavored to show you that we have reason to ascribe every perfection to that being who is himself uncaused, independent & necessarily existing. Now no one can deny that knowledge is a perfection & a natural object of esteem, respect & love & as it is found in some degree in the creature it must be ascribed in an unlimited degree to the creator. All the knowledge which man now possesses or ever will possess, nay, all the most exalted Seraphs know is the gift of God, or it is not just reasoning then to say "he that hath given understanding shall himself not understand"--Besides--In all ages & in all countries we find men disposed to ascribe such knowledge to the deity. This is manifest not only from writings of the heathens, but from the Universal use of an oath in all solemn transactions. Now why should they appeal to deity if they did not believe that he knew their actions? This is a clear belief of a deity who is the avenger of treachery & that from him nothing can be concealed. Indeed without knowledge & wisdom these could be nothing that deserves the name of perfection. If we dare to hazard a conjecture according to our weaker faculties, concerning the objects of the knowledge of the deity we much conclude he knows himself, his creatures & all their constitutions, that he knows all that has existed, that now exists,

or that ever will exist; that he knows every relation of those things of which we now see only so
small a part, & also, that he knows all the events
of necessary causes, as well as of free agents.
Some however have conceived that the future actions
of free agents cannot be known unless they flow from
necessary causes but this never has been proved. We
have indeed no notion of any such power in ourselves
& are at a loss therefore to conceive it to belong
to another, even to Deity but this surely is no reason why it should not belong to him. It never can
be shown to be impossible why future free actions
should not be foreseen & till this is done we have
no reason but to ascribe it to the Supreme Being and
the cause of our being unwilling to allow it even to
him is, that we do not possess it ourselves. If
this however is therefore a sufficient ground to
deny it to him, why not also his creative power. We
know how things already existing may be formed into
various combinations, but how to give existence to
what did not exist before we know not--are we therefore to deny that power to deity? surely not. In
the same manner we know not how the future actions
of free agents can be foreknown & we know not how it
is brought about, but we have this ground to think
that it belongs to Deity, that we by our memory know
actions that are past, yet there is no argument to
show the impossibility of foreseeing future actions
which will not equally apply to Memory & were it not
that we ourselves are endowed with Memory, I apprehend, we would be apt to think that it would be as
impossible as the foreknowledge of future actions.
Some other Philosophers unwilling to deny this power
altogether with Deity attempted to account for it;
but their attempts seems vain & impossible. Dr.
Clarke does it in this way, that we ourselves when
we know the characters of Men, can form some conjecture how they will act in a given situation, so
as we must allow to the Supreme Being a more perfect
acquaintance with the characters of men, hence he
will have a man perfect knowledge how they will act
in any case. This is, I apprehend, reducing the divine prescience to an infinitely sagacious guess.
Besides--it is supposing that men always act according to their characters, which is by no means true.

Some of the Schoolmen, particularly the Jesuits,
in order to account for his foreknowledge, invented
what they called a Scientia Media, that is, not
only a perfect knowledge of all that depends on necessary causes, but also of our events that can happen on any possible situation. With regard to their
Scientia Media there were numberless disputes in the
Schools, which it is [not] my design to enter upon
here--We must also ascribe to the Supreme Being the
possession of his knowledge, without acquiring it,
by labour, it arrived on slow degrees, a knowledge
liable to no error, or Disappointment but which is
certain & unerring & which is the result of his own
Natural perfections.


ENDNOTE for Lect. 81st


11This means that God is everywhere, in the
totality of things and in every part.

77

Lect. 82<sup>d</sup>--

In all these natural attributes of Deity, tho'
we find something analogous to them in the human
Mind, yet we are to consider them as far removed
from all that imperfection with which they are attended. In particular in the case of knowledge, as
formerly noticed, we are not to suppose the knowledge of Deity acquired by slow degrees, or painfull
application, or by inferring one thing from another;
this is altogether inconsistent with the perfections
of the divine Nature. It must be supposed to extend
to all times, past, present or future, nay even to
the thoughts of our hearts, & it is not probable or
conjectural but certain & unerring. This consideration of the divine knowledge ought surely to have
a powerfull influence on our conduct. We know very
well how great an influence the presence of any
character we respect has upon the human Mind. Much
more ought this to have, if we deeply considered
and firmly believed that we were always in the presence of God & that our hearts are always open to him
with whom we have to do. It shows the folly of all
hypocrisy & disguise as we cannot be concealed from
him with whom we are most concerned. It ought to
stiffle also all vain glory & desire to men's applause while at the same it should render us care-
less of their censure or contempt. Let us be more
concerned to appear just & innocent in his sight
who is the best judge of our merit & who will call
us to account.

Another natural attribute to Deity of which we
ought to take notice is his Spirituality, which expresses not so properly what it is, as what it is

79

not. It signifies that his Nature is far removed
from Body or Matter, that it is not confined to
place as material things are, In short, that it
has none of the qualities of matter. We see however in men a great proneness to attribute a visible form to the Deity, usually the human form, as
thinking it the most dignified with which they were
acquainted. This seems to be owing to the weakness
of the human Mind, by which we conceive of other
things as like ourselves & we know & judge by analogy. But of the absurdity of this there is sufficient evidence, if we would consider with any degree of care that the Supreme Being who is eternal,
omnipresent, omniscient & the first cause of all
can never be material. All matter is finite from
its very Nature, or as divided into parts & consists of a variety of parts each of which are distinct & are dependent on the rest & therefore is
incapable of thought for thought never can result
from a composition of different beings. And as
the operations of the Mind are one and indivisible,
so this forms a strong argument that everything
endowed with thought must be immaterial. Tho' the
evidence for this is clear & convincing yet have
men conceived otherwise of the Supreme Being &
such gross conceptions must be considered as the
cause of that general spread of idolatry among the
Heathens. Weak and foolish men conceived the Deity
to inhabit only in their temples, but his presence
is bounded by no such scanty limits for in every
place will the prayer of the humble & acceptable
worshipper be heard by him. Nay, they even imagined, that if they worshipped on the tops of high
mountains, their prayers would be better heard, as
they were nearer heaven than in the valleys.
Strange! That reason should be so corrupted as to
form such mean ideas of the great cause of all;
yet so it is, that we see that they were generally
spread over the heathen world. But every one who
has rational notions of the Deity must conceive,
that he dwells not secure in temples made with
hands but that Universal Nature is his temple &
that his ear is forever open to his Saints wherever
they are placed. It is a natural & a just inference which our Saviour makes from this, that they

o worship him, must worship him in Spirit & Truth
that the homage of the humble & devout which is
st acceptable to him.

Another attribute to Deity is his Unity, that
s he is one & not a number or plurality. We see
w grossly the heathens erred in this, imagining
l the Universe full of Deities, which was entire-
' owing to their mistaken notions of the divine
ture. For had they carefully attended to the at-
ibutes which we have already run over, they might
ve seen that they could not belong to a plurality
t to one. This may be argued from the form &
iform contrivance of the Universe. All appear
der one government, subject to the same laws, &
erefore there must be one Lawgiver. I had occa-
on to mention before a ray of light coming from
e fixed Stars to our system, that is, from the
st distant part of Nature which falls under our
ew, are governed by the same laws of refraction,
flection & inflection, as those produced on the
rface of the Earth or other planets. We see the
w of Gravitation by which various bodies on the
rface of our Earth, gravitate to the Earth ex-
nds also to the Moon & not only to the Moon, but
so to all the Planets of our system, by which
ey gravitate to the Sun & to one another. Thus
om the most distant to the nearest parts of Na-
re all appear one great system, under one governor
subject to the same laws & not according to that
surd idea of the Heathen who conceived a vast
riety of Gods, each of which had their separate
partments, & that they often differed in their
sign & intentions, nay sometimes quarreled &
ught as represented in Homer. But there is no
ch discord under the government of the Deity--
e whole is under one governor & subject to the
me laws. Besides--if we consider this a perfec-
on which our reason tells us to attribute to
ity, then it is impossible to conceive it as
longing to more beings than to one. We have
ready shown that the Deity is eternal & immense
unlimited in all his perfections, now it is im-
ssible to conceive a number of beings endowed
th these. In all cases when we consider number,

81

there must be something to distinguish the individuals of that number from each other; they must be distinguished by time or place or their nature, or some other circumstance; take away all these, the plurality is lost & they really coincide with each other. This reasoning applies to the divine nature. We cannot suppose two beings endowed with these qualities, to be distinguished after the time or place or by their nature or indeed any other circumstance.

I shall only take notice of another Natural attribute of Deity, viz., that he is Immutably Happy. Even the Epicureans gave an eternity of happiness to their deities, but this they conceived to consist in an enjoyment of pleasure without any concern of the affairs of Mortals. Thus write the tenets of Epicurus who placed their happiness in the enjoyment of Sense but reason would lead us to consider it a perfection inherent in the divine Nature & that he who made all & is possessed of all power must be happy in himself. He is therefore called in Scripture the Blessed God, μακάριος, εὐλογητός, meaning properly an object of praise or adoration. One cannot but take notice how from the account now given of the Natural attributes of God, of the perfect correspondence of what we find dictated by reason & the accounts given by the inspired writings. We see in the Old Testament, that Jehovah the Lord God--who revealed himself to the people of Israel, is every where represented as possessed of these qualities of Eternity, Immortality, Power, Perfection, Spirituality & C which from the light of reason we have now ascribed to him. And the same we find in the New Testament & indeed it hardly can be supposed that such rational notions could be formed by a people so ignorant & gross as the Jews were & while the neighbouring nations were all deeply sunk in Idolatry.

Having said these things of the Natural attributes of God, I shall now consider his Moral attributes. There is no branch of knowledge which it concerns us more to know than the moral attributes of the Supreme Being, for, on these depend all our hopes from him & from a knowledge of these will flow

82

out what ever towards him and the devotion we pay
him. If we do not conceive the Supreme Being possessed of moral perfections in the highest degree,
all our services to him will be the effect of fear
& not of true devotion. True devotion can arise
only from a belief that he is the best as well as
the greatest of beings & that our highest Virtue
consists in resembling him as far as our weak faculties allow. By his moral attributes we mean
those which relate to his actions & his conduct,
by which his will & his operations are directed.
He has an active as well as intellectual Nature.
The world was made by him & he upholds & governs
it. And action consists in the exercises of power
& without the desire of acting the power would be
given to no purpose. Therefore to every creature
to whom God has given power, he has given at the
same time the principles of action to prompt them
to the exercise of that power. Thus the instincts,
appetites, & passions of animals all draw them on
to action & the exercise of their power. But besides these encitements to action man is possessed
of a much nobler faculty--the moral faculty--by
which he distinguishes right & wrong in conduct &
distinguishes what he should pursue from what he
should avoid. As by the Eye he perceives colours,
by the Ear sound, the Memory, past events so by
this faculty he perceives what is right--wrong--
what is a subject of approbation, what of censure
or indignation. This I shall have occasion to explain more fully afterwards. I shall there shew
that the qualities of right & wrong which we perceive by the Moral faculty are really qualities
inherent in the moral agent in which we conceive
them to be & not, Merely, as some hold, sensations
in the percipient. Now however we must take it for
granted that there is a real & intrinsic difference
between moral qualities, that gratitude, friendship
& c are in their own Nature more worthy than perfidy, ingratitude & c. Every man who consults his
own breast must be convinced of this. If then
there is a moral character then let us consider if
we have reason to ascribe it to the Deity? Is
there any thing in the Deity analogous to moral
character in Man? Here it ought to be observed,

that there are various principles of action in man
which appear suited only to our dependent Nature &
to a state attended with imperfection--these we
never can suppose to belong to the Supreme Being.
Thus we never possibly can ascribe to him, these
instincts of which we see common to men & the lower
animals, which lead them blindly to certain actions
necessary for such imperfect creatures as we are,
but to a being so perfect as the Supreme Being they
cannot belong. Neither can we ascribe to him these
impulses which men receive from Passions, these
were given to man to supply the defects of reason
& the moral faculty. It is only what belongs to
Man as a rational creature that we must ascribe to
Deity. Now it is manifest that our Reason leads
us to ascribe to him a perfect moral character. In
order to confirm this I observe,

1. Every real excellence in the effect is to
be found in the cause. No reasoning can be more
forcible than this. "He that gave understanding
shall not he understand?", & the same reasoning
leads us to attribute a perfect moral character to
Deity from what we can discover in ourselves. He
who made man capable of acquiring qualities worthy
of esteem, respect & confidence, must surely possess these himself in an infinite degree free from
all the imperfections which accompany them in our
frail Nature. Besides--shall we ascribe to him
knowledge & power & yet deny him righteousness &
truth. Indeed there is no argument which can lead
us to ascribe to him powers & c which will not
equally lead us to ascribe to him those moral qualities which render the being possessed of them
truely excellent & amiable.

2. Another reason why we should ascribe a
perfect moral character to the Deity is, from the
moral government of the World. We see from the
contrivance & administration of things that Virtue
is countenanced & Vice discouraged. Virtue is in
itself rewarded by the approbation of our own Minds;
an approbation is felt from the practice of Virtue
which forms the only sincere enjoyment attainable
in this life. It inspires the mind with confidence

in God & the hopes of a future reward; it affords
a pleasure which never pales on reflection nor is
ever followed by satiety or disgust. This can by
no means be said of the other pleasures of our Nature. They are either momentary in their duration
& often on recollection yeld ground for repentence
& sorrow. Virtue again is countenanced by this
that it tends to enlarge our own power in the world,
to procure respect & good offices for ourselves &
ours. Vice again is punished in the general administration of things as in itself it is attended with
remorse & dread of discovery--by the contempt of men
& the lash of the civil Law.

3. The Voice of Conscience leads us to ascribe
a perfect moral character to the Deity. There is no
sentiment more natural to man than this, Shall not
the judge of all the Earth do right? I had occasion
to observe before trust in the Virtue of God, was
the firm support of injured Virtue & led all men to
the expectation of a future state where a more perfect retribution would take place. This sentiment
of the justice of the Supreme administration is surely what every man feels in himself. I hope there
are none so bad, who commit any bad action without
having some temptation to commit it, some prospect
of interest--some bodily appetite--or something or
other which influences them, even the worst will do
virtue when there is no temptation to the contrary.
Now we cannot suppose the Supreme Being to have any
temptation to do wrong--every creature is his--and
all are in his hands; justly has an inspired Writer
said, "God tempts not any man neither is he tempted."

Having thus briefly shewed that we have reason
to ascribe a perfect moral character to Deity as
well as natural attributes I come now to consider
what notion it is most reasonable to form of the nature of this moral character. Here I observe, that
the only notion we can form of his moral character
is by ascribing to him what appears most excellent
in ourselves separated from all the weaknesses & imperfections of human Nature. We ought to observe
that there are certain virtues grounded on our state
as dependent creatures, liable to danger, error &

misconduct, such as, repentance, contrition, etc.
These are suited to the state of Man, not to the
state of the Supreme Being & can have no place in
him who is exempted from error, danger, disappointment or mistakes. We are then only to ascribe to
him such as imply no weakness or defect, such as
1. goodness & forbearance. 2. Truth and Veracity.
3. Love of and to Virtue and dislike to Vice. 4.
Justice & equity in the administration of things.

  1. Goodness, Mercy & forbearance are evidently implied in a perfect moral character, for without it we can conceive no moral character whatever.
It appears from all the works of creation which are
full of his goodness, that the laws of which the
universe are good & indeed as far as we can know
them they are fitted to promote the interest of his
creatures & to give all that degree of happiness of
which their several natures are capable. These
laws indeed are general & sometimes thro accident
may produce pain, yet the state of man required the
world to be managed by general Laws. If fire should
sometimes burn & sometimes not--if water sometimes
bears(?) him & sometimes not, and so on of other
parts of Nature, it would be impossible without the
longest experience to acquire any prudence in our
conduct. These general laws are necessary & are
well constructed for the purposes of the various
animals which are capable of happiness or misery.
Thus the harms which attend any hurt are necessary
calls to prevent us from neglecting to remedy what
might endanger our health or our life. So the pains
that follow the appetites of hunger & thirst are
necessary to insure supply of meat & drink which we
might otherwise forget. All these general laws
serve as proof of the goodness of the Deity, as they
evidently tend to the wellbeing of his creatures &
the enjoyments of that happiness of which every nature is capable.

  2. Another moral attribute of God is his Truth
and Veracity. There is no attribute belonging to
the Supreme Being, to which we more readily assent
than this & on which we more humbly rely. Some
authors pretend to maintain that in reasoning with

regard to the attributes of God, we ought to reason from nothing but from the appearances we observe in the Universe. Now it might be said that we never experience by means of our reasons of his truth and Veracity. They only have an experience of his truth and Veracity to whom a revelation of his will has been made & who discerned the truth & Veracity in a conduct suited to that Revelation, but they who are left merely to reason can have no such experience-- yet are all men found to believe in the Veracity of the Supreme Being.

We daily experience his goodness, but of his
Veracity we have no such experience; yet is the belief of his Veracity found to be inseparable from
a belief in his existence. Even human authority
previous to experience has a weight with us & let
us suppose that the divine being should please to
communicate anything to us by a revelation. I ask
if any person could doubt of its truth? is it possible any one could think it all a lie?--no man
can entertain such a thought. And the reason of
this seems to be that Truth & Veracity we conceive
as inseparable from a perfect moral character.

3. Love to Virtue & Dislike to Vice is another moral attribute of the Deity. This is likewise
in a perfect moral character for it is impossible
to conceive a being endowed with any considerable
degree of Virtue unless he regards the former and
subdues the latter.

4. Justice. The writers on Jurisprudence
have distinguished Justice into two kinds, Correc-
tive & distributive. The 1. regards our transactions with men when we consider ourselves as on a
level with them, as in making a contract, carrying
on traffic etc. But the 2. is the justice of a
Judge or governor in dispensing rewards & punishments in exact proportion to the merit and demerit
of a person. Now if we ascribe Justice to the Deity
at all, it evidently must be distributive Justice,
that is, a disposition to deal with all his creatures without partiality or prejudice; making all
allowances for those whom his Providence has placed

in a more disadvantageous situation. And in the
final distribution of rewards and punishments justice requires that he should not accept the person
of any one in preference to another of equal merit
& that every alleviation & every aggravation should
have its full power. That the punishment be proportioned to the degree of atrocity in the crime & at
the same time that the rigour of punishment be tempered by clemency in as far as Goodness will permit.
This I think is the best notion we can form of the
moral government of God & this is to be ascribed to
the Supreme Being & it is that character which is
everywhere attributed to him in the Sacred Scriptures, where we are told that "he is no respecter
of persons, but that in every nation he that fears
him & does righteousness shall be accepted of him".
But there are some peculiarities here & which ought
to be attended to when we form a notion of the divine Nature. 1. Tho' it is a dictate both of reason & of conscience that an immoral conduct ought
to be punished, yet they afford us no precept to
determine the measure of that punishment. That
criminal conduct deserves punishment is the voice
of all mens conscience. "No one," says Plato, either of Gods or men dares to say "that Punishment
is not due to the unjust".

οὐδείς οὔτε θεῶν οὔτε ἀνθρώπων εἰπεῖν
τόλμᾳ ὅτι ἀδίκοις κρίνειν μή πρέπει

It is our indignation at this, which makes all so
ready to give their assistance in apprehending male-
factors & in bringing them to punishment. In human
courts, to be sure the judge cannot pass sentence.
As to the real demerit of the criminal, there is
another rule which they use to observe, they are to
judge how far the crime is hurtfull to Society or
Prejudicial to the interest of the Civil Government.
They can judge by no other stand, they know not the
breast, nor what measure of temptation he had or
from what principles he acted. Of this the Supreme
Being is the only judge to him every heart is open
& every circumstance that tends either to alleviate
or to aggravate the guilt. There are many crimes
heinous in their own nature which a human judge

cannot punish at law, as they are not absolutely necessary to preserve the peace of Society. Thus, ingratitude is in itself highly criminal, but it is
not punishable by human laws if there is no injustice done: not that it is not considered as criminal but because it is not considered as necessary
to the preservation of human Society. Xenophon indeed tells us that under Cyrus, the Persians by
their laws punished ingratitude severely. By many
however this account of the Persian constitution is
considered as mostly fiction, & it is certainly true
that never has any instance occured in any well regulated government where ingratitude was held an object of the Civil Law. Further--Reason does not
dictate to us how far clemency should extend to
penitent offenders. Justice certainly requires that
an offender who repents & reforms ought to be otherwise dealt with than one who continues obstinate &
impenitent, but how far this should be carried,
whether they should be remitted altogether, or in
what way or when what terms they should be accepted
reason does not enable us to determine. I have thus
endeavored to shew that we have reason to ascribe a
moral character to the Deity. I shall now consider
some systems that have been advanced by authors of
reputation concerning the attributes of the Deity &
which contradict what I have now held forth as the
fact.

1. I shall consider what has been said by Mr.
Hume, not indeed in his own person but in that of
an Epicurean friend, whose sentiments he has held
forth to us in his Essay on Providence & a future
state & adorned with all the strength of his reasoning & his eloquence, without either adopting or cen-
suring it. He there says, that we have no reason to
[attribute] the Supreme Being wisdom, power, or intelligence, in a higher degree than what we see Manifested in his works; a conclusion evidently grounded
on this, that a cause is exactly proportional, to its
effect, as therefore these marks of wisdom are limited, so we must conclude that this cause, that is,
the perfections of the Deity are limited. "When we
infer any particular cause from an effect, we must
proportion the one to the other, & can never be

allowed to ascribe to the cause any qualities but
what are exactly sufficient to produce the effect.
It is allowed then that the Deity possesses that
degree of wisdom, power & benevolence which appear
in his workmanship, but nothing farther can be
proved, except we call in the assistance of exagger-
ation and flattery to supply the defects of argument & reasoning."[12] I may observe how, that this
notion upon which the argument is grounded, that a
cause is exactly proportioned to the effect, & limited to the effect, may perhaps be true of natural
causes, but as to intelligent causes which operate
freely & voluntary, this maxim is not based on reason. I had occasion to observe formerly that this
word cause is very ambiguous--sometimes it signifies
only some concomitant circumstances & sometimes even
the Name of the cause is given to the Law of Nature
itself. This is an important sense, but tho' from
the use of Language we cannot avoid it, yet ought
we to be cautious lest we be imposed on by the am-
biguity of terms. In the proper & strict sense of
the word we understand by cause, any agent with power to produce the effect & will to produce it. When
we say cold is the cause of freezing in water, cold
is here used in a vague and improper sense; cold is
only a negation of heat & cannot be the cause of
anything. But that is a cause of an effect which
has power to produce it. We say too heat is the
cause of the liquor rising in the thermometer--here
heat is used in a vague sense. But when we apply
this maxim to intelligent beings, that the cause is
proportional to the effect, it will be found to hold
neither in reason nor in the common judgement of Men.
Suppose I should ask a man, on a journey, pray which
is the road to Edinburgh? and he returns me a perti-
nent answer. Here the Understanding of the Man is
the cause. The answer is the effect. Now, perhaps
I never spoke to the Man before--I know nothing about
him. Am I therefore to conclude that his understanding just enabled him to answer my question & neither
more nor less? surely this would be absurd--the natural conclusion is, that he has such a degree, how
much more I do not know. Again if I converse with
anyone half an hour upon Antient history & find that
his knowledge is accurate, full & well digested.

Shall I say that this man knows no more than what I have heard him express? by no means--I am to conclude that he knows not only what he has expressed but much more. So it is with regard to his goodness.--If I had stood in need of the benevolent assistance of a friend & that I found him always prompt to bestow his favours, do I conclude that he has merely that degree which he has manifested to me, & that I have experienced all his Stock?-- It appears then that this maxim of Mr. Hume's, when applied to voluntary causes is neither self-evident nor consistent with our reasoning about causes in common Life. But then it may be said, that we can consider the Supreme Being, as possessed only of that degree of choices of power & wisdom etc. which we see displayed in his works. This indeed is Mr. Hume's reasoning, but it is evidently grounded on the Supposition, that there is no argument for the perfections of Deity except what is drawn (from) those indications of perfection which we see in his works. This is no doubt one topic from which we do reason on the Subject, as Hume supposes it to be. We conceive that there is real force in our reasoning from the Necessary Existence of Deity & his unlimited Perfections. It has already been shewed by clear arguments that that being who exists without a cause, or a beginning, exists necessarily so that it is impossible to him not to exist or not to have such a degree of power, wisdom & goodness as is manifested in his works. Nor can it be said that necessary existence has a connection with one degree of power which it has not with another. When we consider a being possessed of necessary existence we can see no connection he has with one portion of time more than another, that therefore his duration is from everlasting to everlasting. We conceive him to have no greater connection with one part of Space than another, that therefore he is omnipresent. In like manner when we conceive him as endowed with one degree we must consider [him] as perfect of every degree as there is no connection between necessary existence & one degree which is not with another. This reasoning applies to all the other attributes of God. I endeavored to shew formerly that he has

93

endowed with <u>unlimited</u> Perfection, from the consideration of his necessary existence. We cannot avoid
ascribing different degrees of perfection to different objects, thus, we prefer a plant to a clod of
earth--an animal to a plant--a rational to an irra-
tional animal & a being endowed with the highest degrees of perfection is the most perfect we can conceive. Now if there really is such a thing as perfection & imperfection we cannot help thinking that
there is more perfection in the cause than in the
effect, nor would the Deity have given us ideas of
perfection beyond what he really himself possesses.
We may observe that the reasoning of Mr. Hume's
tends greatly to lessen the perfection of Deity--to
reduce them from infinite to finite & bring them to
a level with our own, at least, to set them not so
far above us as that a comparison may be drawn between the excellencies of Men & the excellency of
God. Shocking thought! Presumptuous man! does
think with the short line of thy understanding to
search the unfathomable wisdom of God? It is difficult, indeed to say whether pride, impiety or presumption are more conspicuous in the man who makes
the bold attempt; the man whose boasted understanding is unable to discover how one particle of matter
adheres to another. Indeed the idea is so singular,
that I once imagined that either Mr. Hume or his
Epicurean friend must have been the inventors of it,
but I find that Milton, long before Hume's time, has
attributed it to Lucifer, who gives the same reason
to encourage his associates in rebellion against
their Maker but they were convinced of their error
by this event.

"                              So much the stronger
        proved
He with his thunder; & till then who knew
The force of those dire arms? whom I now
of force believe almighty, since no less
than such could have o'erpowered such force
        as ours"13

    I now proceed to consider another subject con-
cerning the moral attributes of Deity, which has
come from a different quarter but equally unfriendly

94

to Religion & Virtue. I mean Lord Bolingbroke, it
has been advanced indeed by Mr. Hobbes before & we
find it adopted by Mr. Hume in a Posthumous work of
his on Natural Religion. He admits that there must
be a first cause possessed of power, wisdom, & the
other natural attributes which we have ascribed to
him, but maintains that we know nothing of his moral
attributes or the principles of his actions; when we
talk of his goodness, Mercy, or justice, we use,
says he, words without meaning. This system strikes
at the root of all Religion, for if the Moral attributes of Deity are taken away, we can have no foundation for all the homage we pay him, or for all the
hopes we have from him. He who believes that the
Lord is just in all his ways & holy in all his works,
this justice & judgement are the habitations of his
throne & that mercy & truth forever go before his
face will of consequence believe that real Virtue &
real excellence consist solely in our resemblance to
him, a consideration which gives them an authority
they could not otherwise have. But this system cuts
all of the sinews of virtuous conduct, robs it of
all its splendor & rests it on a very weak & slippery
foundation. We certainly, however, have the same
reason to ascribe justice & goodness to the Deity as
power & intelligence nor is there the least ground
to think his moral attributes more incomprehensible
than his natural attributes. We acknowledge that
our ideas of all the attributes & of the being of
Deity are inadequate, but this is no reason why we
should not have as distinct a notion of his goodness,
justice & truth as of his power & intelligence.
There are some vestiges of both in the human Mind &
of the one our notions are as clear as of the other.

¹²As in the case of the Milton quote below, the text suggests that the sentences appear consecutively in the original; they do not.

The essay quoted appeared as Section XI in Hume's Enquiry Concerning the Human Understanding. I have not looked at all editions, but in the edition of 1777, the last revision Hume made before he died in 1776, the first sentence begins a paragraph. It is followed by an example. "A body of ten ounces raised in any scale may serve as a proof, that the counterbalancing weight exceeds ten ounces; but can never afford a reason that it exceeds a hundred." There follows more argument, another full paragraph, and then a third paragraph that begins, "Allowing, therefore, the gods to be the authors of the existence or order of the universe; it follows that they possess that precise degree of power, intelligence, and benevolence which appears in their workmanship . . ." etc. It may be that there is an earlier edition in which the passage is as quoted; I cannot confirm this.

See: Enquiries Concerning the Human Understanding and Concerning the Principles of Morals by David Hume, edited by L. A. Selby-Bigge (London: Oxford University Press, 1972), pp. 136-137.

¹³This quotation is from John Milton's Paradise Lost, of course, Book I. But the lines are not consecutive. The first part is lines 92-94. The rest is a parenthesis, "(whom I now . . . as ours)", lines 143-145.

Lect. 84$^{th}$

We can have no greater degree of testimony for
the truth of anything than the testimony of our
Senses & of these qualities which God has given us;
by these we discover that some propositions are
true and others false & he who [has] a conviction
of the imperfection of his faculties, presumes to
call in question their information, must remain a
Sceptic for ever there is no remedy for it.  Now
our judgement of right & wrong is as certain as our
judgement of true and false & to suppose that the
supreme being [to] have another standard of measur-
ing them than we, that he thinks morally ill what
we think morally good & the contrary, is as absurd
as to say that he has a different conception of
what is true and false.  For it is no less evident
that goodness, justice, humanity, etc., are intrin-
sically better than their contrary, than that 2+2
make 4, it must surely be allowed that a being of
infinite understanding & intelligence can discern
these moral relations as well as we.  If the difference between moral right & wrong are distinguished by an human Mind, much more so by him whose
understanding is infinite.  It is an eternal & im-
mutable truth that Virtue in human Nature is amica-
bly respectable & deserving approbation, that Vice
on the contrary is an object of disapprobation, dislike & demerit.  When we judge so we judge according
to the truth, the Supreme Being must be allowed always to judge according to truth, therefore they
must appear so to him as to the human mind.

Having considered these two theories, which
tend wholly to overturn the attributes of the Deity

I now proceed to consider some hypotheses whose authors in themselves were not unfriendly to Religion,
but which have been advanced in order to render our
notion of the divine attributes more conceivable &
to give such impressions of them as are most agreeable to truth. The first of these I shall take notice of is what is commonly called the Bellestan
(?)[14] theory, of this I shall now give some account
& offer a few remarks upon it. Whoever wants to see
it more fully explained may consult Leibnitz, in his
Theodicè, who has adopted it. It has been also
adopted by others, as that which gave the best account of the origin of Evil & the most amiable representations of the divine perfections & administration. According to this system, the Supreme Being
from all eternity, by his infinite understanding saw
all the possible constitutions of worlds which could
be & their various qualities. Among all the possible systems that could be he would choose that in
which there was the greatest sum of happiness upon
the whole. He then from his infinite understanding
& his perfect goodness, constituted the present system as that which contained the greatest possible
sum of happiness on the whole & that all the divine
attributes consist in directing all things to produce
the greatest degree of good on the whole. This system leads to form a particular notion of the divine
attributes. It is conceived, that though we give
different names to the moral attributes of Deity,
such as justice, truth, & righteousness, yet that
they may all be resolved into one are only different
modifications of his goodness or benevolence, that
is, a disposition to promote the greatest degree of
happiness on the whole in the Universe. Some others
since Leibnitz have followed this system & particularly a divine among the Dissenters in England, whose
name is commonly thought to be Boyce, in a pamphlet
entitled Divine Benevolence, in which he has endeavored to shew that all the moral attributes we ascribe
to Deity are only modifications of benevolence, or
benevolence considered in particular lights. We see
that according to this system, there is supposed in
Deity, no love of Virtue, or dislike of Vice, than
as they tend to promote the happiness or misery of
the beings in the world. That a desire of promoting

the happiness of all is the only principle of his
action & gave rise to his Laws & the government
which he exercises. By this system, it is thought
the best account of the origin of Evil, both natural & moral can be given. They think that all the
Evil we see in the World is a necessary ingredient
in a system in which we see the greatest possible
good; it was proper then to admit it & if we remove
it an equal proportion of happiness is at the same
time removed. We cannot help thinking this a theory
of the divine attributes, but it is a theory which
tho' well intended has no sufficient arguments to
enforce it, nor does it after all give us any clearer notions of the attributes of God than we had before. For, 1. as we can only form a just notion
of moral character in Deity from what appears most
perfect in moral character among human creatures
when separated from all the imperfections with
which they are attended in us, so I Conceive that
goodness alone is far from making a perfect moral
character in Man. We cannot conceive a moral character without a regard to Virtue & a Dislike to Vice.
To make the only principle of action in man to produce the happiness of others is to degrade his Nature. This tho' a necessary branch of Virtue is not
the whole of it. There is no reason why the whole
attributes of the Deity then should be resolved into
one -- 2. Tho' by this system we have the greatest
possible sum of happiness, yet does it carry very
uncomfortable prospects along with it & which appear
very far from being agreeable to the Truth. For it
supposes that in this system evil has a necessary &
fatal connection with good & that it could not be
removed even by divine Power. This is to suppose a
Fate superior to the human being, which necessarily
connects evil with the greatest possible sum of happiness. Likewise--we see that this system leads to
the Necessity of all human actions, which indeed was
maintained by Leibnitz & the other patrons of this
system, because it was necessary that every part
should be adjusted to produce the greatest degree of
happiness on the whole. Now if our authors affirm
that the greatest possible sum of good could not be
without that degree of evil we observe then they admit that there is a necessary & total connection

between the one & the other. If however they do not
adopt this system of a fated necessity, if they admit these moral attributes, which we conceive as
real perfections then we have no reason that evil is
necessarily connected with good, nor is it necessary
to reduce all his moral attributes to one class.
Perfect Virtue in Man consists not in a desire to
promote the happiness of the Universe, without any
regard to truth, any love of Virtue, or dislike of
Vice, now we form our notions of the Divine by the
human character, if then we ascribe there a perfect
human character, they must be attributed equally to
the Deity--Some again conceive that the attributing
different moral attributes to the Deity is inconsistent with the simplicity & unity of his Nature which
we ought to ascribe to an infinitely perfect being.
But in this there is little force. Our conceptions
of the Supreme Being are undoubtedly inadequate, but
such as these notions are they are the result of our
faculties, & their imperfections must remain with us
till all our faculties are enlarged. We find too
the Sacred Writers ascribing to Deity not only perfect goodness & benevolence but also of a perfect
purity who cannot behold iniquity; a God of truth in
whom is no iniquity: these representations lead us
to conceive of a moral character in the Supreme Being, as we conceive it in a human Being but without
the imperfections of humanity. Indeed if this were
not the case, & if these attributes to which we give
names in man had not the same meaning when we turn
to God, we would speak without understanding, & could
reason no way with regard to them.

    There have been others who thro' a love of a
simplicity & to reduce the divine attributes to what
they think consistent with the Unity in divine Nature, have included all under Divine rectitude &
Divine Wisdom. But it does not appear that by reducing then all under one word we make the notion
of them any clearer. Before I leave this subject
we may consider a little the original Evil, a subject which has given rise to many theories some of
them absurd & others which tend to darken it rather
than throw light upon it. All the evil we see in
the world may be considered in two different lights.

1. As giving rise to objections by some who are unfriendly to Religion, against a good government of
the world & as a topic from which atheists draw arguments against a good administration of this world.
2. as a phenomenon giving occasion to the wit &
ingenuity of philosophers & divines to exorcise themselves in accounting for its origin & why permitted
under a good government.

All evil has by some been reduced to 3 classes,
1. the evils of imperfection, 2. Evil which they
call natural Evil, 3. Moral evil.

1. By evil of imperfection is meant no more
than this, that in the creatures we observe, there
is not that degree of perfection which they might
have had. That is, that a man might have been much
more perfect, he might have been an angel, a brute
might have been a rational being & a plant might have
been a brute animal--this however is not an evil, it
is only a less degree of good. 2. There is Natural
evil, that is that suffering & pain which we see en-
dured by beings in the Universe. 3. Moral Evil,
that is, the violation of the laws of Virtue by moral & reasonable agents. When this evil & Imperfection is offered as an objection against the good administration of things we ought to observe 1. that
objections which have equal force against any possible system which can be contrived, have no force
at all & are therefore to be rejected. Now with regard to the evil of imperfection it appears impossible that any system can be made free from this objection. It therefore can have no force. Suppose a
world twice, nay two thousand times more perfect
than ours still the objection remains, still they
could have been more perfect. Again--as to natural
evils, they are brought as against a good administration of things, it may be denied that they answer
many good ends. We see that it is by natural evil
that men are trained unto wisdom & prudence in their
conduct. Whether men could have been trained to that
degree of wisdom, freedom & Virtue without these
means we are not competent judges & cannot possibly
determine, but from the present constitution of
things we see they are necessary to our acquiring

any prudence or wisdom, or patience or resignation. Besides, that as far as we perceive they are necessary consequences of good general laws. I shewed before that it was necessary for the constitution of rational creatures that they should be governed by general laws, for without these they never could pursue any means to the attainment of an end. And in a world governed by general laws occasionally evils will happen. If gravitation is a good general law & necessary to the presentation of our world, yet by this means(?) houses may fall & crush the inhabitants. It may be observed 3. that we cannot determine what proportion this evil bears to the sum of the enjoyment of God's creatures. We see only a small part & can't judge of the whole of the Universe. If a man who was a stranger to Britain should land upon any corner of it & from that form an opinion of the whole, how uncertain must his Guidance be? Next. Moral Evil, this means the misconduct of rational beings & has also been objected to a good administration of all things, by the Atheists. In order to judge of this let us consider what properly can be said to be God's doing & what is not to be considered in that light. If on one hand we suppose man not to be a free agent then every event good or bad is to be considered as God's doing, and the actions of the worst men are equally imputable to Deity as the rising or setting of the Sun. But if on the other hand, we suppose God to have given Man a Certain Sphere of Power, then the actions done in consequence of this are Men's only & not God's. There is no maxim more evident than that what's the action of one agent cannot be the action of another. If men then are voluntary agents no argument can be drawn from them either for or against the Supreme administration. What then can properly be said to be God's doing from which we may judge of his moral character? Here I observe 1. every creature is made by God & has its qualities from him, therefore there are to be ascribed to him. 2. What are the necessary consequences of what constitutions are also properly his doing & operation. This is no less agreeable to reason than to the Sacred Scriptures. He made the Sun, Moon & Stars, he made a place for the Sea, he feeds the young Lions,

& hears the savage cry and all of these he does either by means of some subordinate agent, or by his own immediate power. 3. to him we must ascribe the lot in which we are placed by his Providence with all its advantages and disadvantages. By such a connection with fellow men we are indeed liable to be sometimes hurt, this is a consequence of our situation. But such injurious actions are not to [be] attributed to God; he indeed gave the power, but they proceed from an abuse of that power. All moral evil then is not properly the doing of God but of men, who by abusing their power are liable to misery & are then justly punished for their misconduct.

It appears then that the objection against a good administration of all things brought either from the evils of imperfection, natural evil or moral evil have no force. I now proceed to consider evil as affording room for exorcising (?) the evil & ingenuity of philosophers & divines to account for its origin & why it was permitted to exist in the world--this I shall speak of in my next Lecture--


ENDNOTE for Lect. 84th


14I confess this word is new to me. It clearly refers, however, to a proposed solution to the problem of evil which emphasizes the goodness of God to the neglect (in Reid's view) of His justice.

103

Lect. 85<sup>th</sup>

That the system, called the Bellestan(?), was
invented for the purpose of enabling us to comprehend more easily the moral attributes of Deity, the
origin of evil & the end for which it was permitted
to prevail, is not to be doubted. But we must always judge that these authors who pretend to unrav-
el all the mysteries of divine Providence & like
Ariadne's thread, pretend to lead us thro' all the
turning & winding of this great Labyrinth, however
much they deserve praise for their zeal, deserve
little for their prudence or modesty. To comprehend the plan of the Universe & all the laws by
which it is governed exceeds the utmost extent of
human genius. Presumptuous man that thou art!
wouldst thou vainly wish to be Privy Counsellor to
the Almighty, thou who are unable to comprehend
half the wisdom displayed in the meanest works of
God. Consider the puny worm that crawls beneath
thy feet & licks the dust of the Earth, doest thou
know the end for which it was made? the useful
purposes it serves to thee & to other animals?
Canst thou unfold its structure? no man can--Here
the art of the skillful anatomist is baffled; the
Physiologist, the Philosopher are put to shame--
Shall we then vainly seek to comprehend the whole
who know not how one particle of matter adheres to
another & how one body communicates motion to another. As soon may a mite comprehend the structure
of an Orrery or unfold a system of Legislature, as
we, the structure & plan of the Universe. We see
indeed in every thing around us, in the curious
structure of all our Bodies & Minds, means excellently adapted to certain ends, we see a profusion

105

of wisdom & power displayed, but all that falls under our view is only an inconsiderable part of the
whole. Any man who would read a few pages of the
Iliad of Homer, would have good reason to conclude
that he was a very great Poet, but from such a small
specimen no man that was not a fool, would pretend
to describe the plan of the whole or the manner in
which it was concluded. In the like manner from the
little we know of the works of God we have good reason to ascribe to him, goodness wisdom & power, but
there is neither wisdom nor modesty in ourselves,
when from the little we see we think to describe the
plan of the whole. In this respect the Bellestan(?)
theory & all others formed to explain the ends of
phenomena we see in the Universe may be compared to
the various theories of the Earth which we have had
by different authors. Many attempts have been made
to explain the present appearances of things, of
mountains, valleys, minerals, etc. different strata
& layers of earths, these extraneous bodies, animal
& vegetable found at great depths in the Earth & so
on. Many ingenious authors have exercised their art
to invent a hypothesis to solve all these appearances.
According[ly] we find some attributing all to the
universal Deluge, in which every thing was displaced
torn up & tost about & hence that mixture of marine
bodies on the tops of mountains & so on which is to
be found. Others again think the Morllu deluge insufficient for this purpose, and ascribe mountains &
all these phenomena to the eruptions of Earthquakes
& Volcanoes. Some again are of opinion that the
whole Earth was originally covered with Sea & as
some places gradually wore away then others were
left higher & became mountains. Others, account for
them by a gradual decrease of the waters, by which
more & more ground was gradually left dry. Such are
some of the conjectures about these appearances &
what do they amount to? They are only the dreams of
Speculative men. Hence it is that every new theorist
easily confutes the system of his predessors & erects
one equally flimsy in its stead, which falls also
before them that come after him. Now if this is the
case in this instance, how can we expect to discover
the plan of the Universe, of which we know so little
& make so small a part. Hypotheses, indeed, of any

kind, as I have often mentioned to you, brought to explain the appearances of things, are only the whims of a fanciful Imagination & have always a higher probability of being found false & futile than true. As well may a child understand the various beauties or defects of the British constitution, or settle the balance of power in Europe, as we comprehend the plan of the great empire of God. In a word so weak a construction is our understanding that even in a human production, we meet with objections which we cannot answer & difficulties which we are unable to resolve. In the meanest of Nature's works we are presented with difficulties which the short line of our understanding cannot sound. What presumption then is it, to attempt to discover the end, for which the Universe was formed & all the different parts made subservient to the whole. In what we see no doubt we perceive manifest indications of wisdom and power & goodness from which we may conclude that these attributes belong to the author of all, but how ridiculous to think of comprehending the ends of the whole when we cannot comprehend the end of one of the meanest creatures. I observed before, that one from reading a few pages of the Iliad might have room to admire the abilities of the Poet but surely he who pronounced from that with regard to the plan of the whole would justly be stigmatized as a fool, and if we cannot comprehend the works of Men how shall we pretend to comprehend the works of God? In what we see there are proofs of wisdom & power, but all is far above our comprehension. He who takes it for granted that he is equal to the arduous task of unfolding the laws of the Universe, will infallibly make blundering work of it & instead of solving objections by his theory he will rather create more & indeed we find that the objections of irreligious men are commonly made to these theories, which are not framed from a just observation of Nature, but are the creations of fancy & therefore more easily demolished —— —— —— —— Thus have I offered what I had to say with regard to the attributes of the Supreme Being & shall only make one observation upon the whole and that is, that as the generality of men are little fitted for reasoning on subjects of this kind, as very strange perversions of sentiment concerning the truths of Natural Religion, have prevailed among the heathens, tho' from what we have now seen, all things appear to be under one government & subject to the same laws, yet was the opinion of a plurality universal among them. The Immensity, eternity & unlimited Perfection of the Supreme Being, are necessarily connected with his necessary existence, yet the deities of the heathens were all conceived to have had a beginning, to have each his different department assigned him, and to be limited with the faults & even vices of humanity. Such were their gross conceptions of their Gods nor was all the philosophy of the polished Greeks & Romans able to root them out. We must observe at the same time, that there was one nation, I mean the Jews, who had more rational notions of the Supreme Being & of his attributes, notions perfectly agreeable to the dictates of reason as we have explained them. Now we can hardly suppose that a nation, barbarous as the Jews were, should have their reasoning powers more refined on this subject than their neighbors, without a Revelation from the Father of Lights. This then may teach us of how Great importance it is, for [us] to attain proper notions of the Deity & his attributes, since so many of mankind, have wandered so far from the truth & so contrary to what reason would dictate to them.

I now proceed to consider the Works of God, which is the last branch of this division of our Course. These have commonly by writers been referred to two heads. 1. The Creation of things, & 2. His subsequent government of them.

1. With regard to Creation, that is, the giving existence to what had no existence before, we do not find this to have been the opinion of the heathen philosophers. We do not find that they conceived there was any such power, as the giving existence to what had no existence before. They conceived that as there must be an eternal contriver & artificer of the Universe, so there must be an eternal matter necessarily existing of which all things were made. The Platonists & Pythogoreans,

who are allowed to have formed the justest & most
rational conceptions of the Deity, yet we find that
all of these sects maintain three eternal first principles. 1. an eternal cause is the Maker of all
things. 2. An eternal matter of which all things
were made. 3$^d$. an eternal idea or model according
to which all things were made. What seems to have
led them to this error is, that Creation is a work
totally dissimilar to any thing which is within the
compass of human power. The Supreme being has given
us the power of compound[ing] & decompounding what
already exists but in us there is no vestage of the
power of Creation, we in no instance can give being
to what had it not before. All the works of human
power extend neither to creation nor annihilation
& this operation being so far beyond our own power
we are unwilling therefore to allow it even to the
Deity. But this is weak reasoning & if we duly ex-
ert our powers of reason, we will see it more probable that finite things must have their existence
from the hand of the first cause of all. Indeed
from the properties of matter it appears impossible
that it should be eternal or necessarily existing.
What exists necessarily must exist every where & in
all points of duration but omnipresence & ubiquity
belongs not to Matter from its nature it is limited
to one place, it cannot then be necessarily existing.
And if we acknowledge that the Supreme Being gave
existence to beings of a superior nature even to
natural Beings, it appears silly to attribute necessary existence to the meanest of the creatures of
God.

March 2$^d$, 1780.

Lect. 86<sup>th</sup>    March 3<sup>d</sup>, 1780

When speaking of Creation we may take notice of
a theory which has been advanced by some Theologians,
with a good design no doubt, but which seems to draw
dangerous consequences along with it, it is this,
that the preservation of God's creatures is a per-
petual & constant recreation, & that therefore from
the very nature of created beings, they must every
moment fall into annihilation if not thus reproduced
as it were.  This is no doubt intended to represent
more forcibly to us our entire dependence on the Supreme Being, but it must not be taken in too strict
a sense, otherwise, our personal identity would be
lost, for if what exists this moment is annihilation,
then, what exists the next moment is not the same
with that which is no more, nor can it be accountable for its actions.  Indeed it is impossible that
we can form a notion of what is necessary to continue
creatures in existence, we know not what it is as we
know not the power which gave it being but we cannot
I apprehend reasonably conclude that it is the same
with creation.  A very ingenious Philosopher, as well
as pious divine gives us his sentiments on this subject.  I mean Dr. Isaac Watts, you will find them in
his Philosophical Essays, Essay 11th Section 4 to
which I refer you.  What he says there is perfectly
agreeable to reason & good sense & I shall only add,
that this notion of preservation, being a continual
creation, is destructive of all personal identity &
of consequences of it, accountableness of human actions ———  ——— I shall now consider the government of the Supreme Being which has been distinguished into two kinds, viz. 1.  His Natural government
& 2.  His Moral.  On this subject we ought to speak

111

witn reserve & modesty & draw conclusions only from
what our faculties are fully able to reach without
pretending to form any conceptions with regard to
the plan of the whole. According to the theory of
Leibnitz the world was so made as to need no operation of the Deity for its government; that every
thing had such power implanted in it at its first
constitution, that produce all subsequent changes
without any interposition of the Supreme Being &
therefore he considered every interposition of the
Deity as a miracle. This is a theory which had many
admirers but seems to have no foundation in truth
or in reason. It may be observed, that he differs
from the common meaning affixed to the word miracle.
It is not every interposition of Deity that constitutes an action miraculous; it is only actions done
in express violation of the usual fixed laws of Nature in order to attest a divine omniscience. Thus
the raising from the dead a man who has been four
days in his grave & what body is become putrid by a
single word, this is a miracle as it is contrary to
the Laws of Nature. But that every interposition
of Deity is a miracle cannot be admitted. We see
indeed that the world is governed by general Laws,
but do not laws require an agent to execute them &
to produce effects according to them. Laws are not
agents, they are only rules according to which an
agent operates, the laws of Nature then suppose an
agent to operate according to these laws, but whether the Supreme Being executes these immediately or
by subordinate beings is beyond the reach of our
comprehension. Besides, it cannot ever be shewn
that this system of Leibnitz's is even possible.
He endeavors to illustrate it from the structure of
a clock. If, says he, a workman should make a clock
that perpetually goes on of itself without needing
any future interposition, any mending or reparation
this surely would be a more perfect machine than the
one that required the hand of the artificier to be
continually employed in regulating its motions &
preventing it from going wrong. Now, all the works
of God are surely perfect, the Universe then being
the work of God must be perfect & therefore need no
future interposition of the power to direct or support it. This similitude Leibnitz relied on as being

conclusive, but if examined carefully it will be
found to fail much. The workman indeed fashioned
the materials & arranged them in a certain order
but was he the author of these materials, or did
he give them these powers by which the work is carried on? did he give to matter that cohesive power
between the particles which is necessary to the
clock's being formed? did he give it that tendency
to descend or gravitate to the Earth by which the
motion is caused & which if it ceases, the machine
must immediately stop? All that he does is only
to apply certain powers, but it is nature & not him
that confers these powers. Between these two then
there is no similitude, neither is there a greater
beauty in the system, than if we believed that all
things are governed by a Supreme Being, or by some
subordinate agent employed by him. Why should it
be thought unworthy of Deity to preserve by his
care, these natures he formed at first by his power? Indeed, it is unsuitable to the principles of
Philosophy or the Sacred Scripture which everywhere
represent him as the kind preserver of all his work.
With regard to the rules of the Natural government
of God, it appears 1. He governs all things by general Laws, as far as we can judge. He may however
conceive the Supreme Being to have fashioned all
things occasionally, but this is inconsistent with
the moral government of his rational creatures.
For were not all carried on by fixt laws they never
could require any prudence, wisdom or forethought--
it is by general laws therefore that the Supreme
Being governs & in so doing his wisdom and goodness
are conspicuous. These are called Physical Laws,
in order to distinguish them from what are called
Moral Laws by which is meant, those rules which
ought to regulate the conduct of rational & moral
agents. The former were appointed by the almighty
himself & are executed by him, they are therefore
seldom violated & as I just now observed, were not
the world governed thus men never could acquire any
prudence in their conduct thro' life tho' he could
as easily have done it by particular volitions. 2.
These general laws which interest us most are made
obvious to the experience of all & are soon perceived by all. Thus, that fire will burn them,

113

that water will drown, that bodies all gravitate. Such then as are necessary to be known are obvious to all, but there are others again more hidden which are left to the sagacity of man to investigate by his reason & industry. These which are commonly called Laws of Nature & which are the first principles of Natural Philosophy, no more properly deserve that title, than many of these laws which are obvious to the Vulgar, only the one is more hidden than the other. Those which are necessary to all are made obvious to all, but those again which are less necessary, though of use to enlarge human knowledge & human power are left to be discovered by our own sagacity & labour. These indeed have already gone great lengths; by them we have discovered why Planets roll on their orbits & the Comets are retained in their circles & how far human genius may carry us no man can say. There is still ample room for the exercise of our talents from the beginning to the end of our existence & every new discovery we make tends to widen the sphere of our power & activity. For it is by means of our knowledge of the Laws of Nature that we can bring about any end by using the properest means. It is by a knowledge of the laws relating to the fruits of the Earth that the husbandman knows when to plow & when to sow. By a knowledge of these the Navigator totally traverses the wide Ocean, and, in a word, it is by a knowledge of these that every human art is carried on. The more then this knowledge is increased, the more will our power in these be enlarged. In the investigation of these our talents find a manly & rational exercise & our labour seldom fails to be rewarded by the advantages that follow it. 3. In the government of God we see brutes and infants directed by other inferior principles which supply the want of reason, by instincts, appetites, & passions. Were not the child directed by instinct it must inevitably perish. Of itself it would never know that food was necessary to its preservation, far less, that that food was contained in the breast of the Mother & to be sucked out by its mouth, yet in all this, it is directed by instinct. Nothing shews more evidently the wisdom & superintendence of a Supreme Being than such instincts. We are unable indeed to discern

114

the proximate (or physical?) cause of them, but their effects we see, & find that they are admirably fitted for this purpose for which they were intended. Likewise--we may observe, that men are directed by many inferior principles which supply the room of Reason & assist us in our progress in Virtue & moral goodness. That men were intended to make progress in Virtue is obvious, but the progress which is made by the greatest number is small & inconsiderable. Society of consequence could not subsist, if men were not directed by other principles of actions to the same course to which Virtue itself would naturally lead them. We say thus, that Society may subsist not only among those which are Virtuous, but even among those that are really bad, till they are corrupted in such a degree as we have few examples of in the history of the World. Men by means of their social passions, of natural affection, & c, tho' possessed of very little Virtue are yet prompted to that very path which Virtue if followed would point out. It is the duty of the parent to rear, educate and protect their children, but even this done only from principles of Virtue, I am afraid that in the greatest number, we would find it neglected, to prevent this, we find implanted in every breast a natural affection, a δοργη [15], as the Greeks called it, which operates on all & produces those effects which Virtue ought to produce. So in like manner the social affections, of gratitude, compassion, natural affection to relations & the Love of our Country operate on the good & the bad & supply the defects of Virtue. By these is Society supported & that whether the members of it are good or bad, virtuous or vicious, wise or foolish. We see too principles implanted in Mankind which tend to our improvement, in arts, knowledge & good habits. Of these we may take notice of that principle of <u>Activity</u> in children which is instinctive & necessary for their acquiring habits for their improvement in knowledge. Even the perfect use of our Senses is to be acquired by habit & practice. Children thus by their desire of seeing every object with their eyes & handling with hands, improve them greatly & before they come to the years of understanding have them in perfection. I took an opportunity formerly also to shew that even

our perceptions were mostly acquired & we see that
Nature has fitted us with instincts fitted to acquire them. Credulity too is evidently implanted
in our Nature for our improvement. It is a natural
law of our Nature, that even before we ourselves
knew the importance of knowledge, we listen with
patience to what is told us & swallow it down with
security by which means we acquire knowledge before
we could learn it by our own discoveries. The imi-
tative principle in Man was also intended too for
progress in improvement. By this he is led to imitate what is done by others & thus easily acquires
habits of great importance to him. We know from
Experiments that have been made, that it is even
possible to teach deaf people to speak & pronounce
articulate sounds tho' they have it not in their
powers to imitate these in others, by instructing
them how to form the particular organs for the various sounds. This is no doubt a great art & requires
great labour & attention. But the same difficulty
would be found in every one who learns articulate
sounds & language, if it were not from the powers of
imitating these sounds by others. We may observe
also, that these principles given for self defense,
called Malevolent Passions tho' intended to promote
our improvement & happiness in Society, yet from
their very nature have checks to prevent their ex-
cess. They are attended with an uneasy feeling
which is an admonition to indulge them no further
than what is necessary for our own good & the good
of those to whom we wish well. We see by the constitution of things too that industry is encouraged as
necessary to our subsistence. It is undoubtedly intended that Man should earn his bread by the sweat
of his brows, that he should provide the necessities
of life by his labour & for this we see him adapted.
And while we are prompted to action by the infamy,
poverty & contempt which follows indolence & sloth,
yet we are warned of the same, by a langour and lassitude which attends too violent exertions of our
powers to take alternate repose. From all these observations, we may remark, that there are some obvious general rules of God's Natural Government which
are admirably fitted to the condition of Man in this
world.

Having said these things with regard to the
Natural Government, I come now to the <u>Moral Government of God</u>. In the former he acts as a man does
with his property; he disposes it in every particular as his wisdom & skill direct him:   therefore
whatever is done in the Natural world, may properly
be ascribed to God as his doing, such as the Motion
of the Moon, of all the Planets, the ebbing and flow-
ing of the Seas & so on:   these all are the operations of the Deity, & the general rules according to
which they are produced are called <u>Physical laws</u>;
they are the rules to which he adheres & which of
consequence are never transgressed.   But in his <u>Moral
Government</u>, he acts like a Legislator, who proposes
rules of conduct to his subjects & as they obey or
disobey them so may they expect his favour or dis-
pleasure.   As to the inanimate creation it is necessarily passive & can be subject to no laws.   The
brute animals again, tho' they possess a degree of
power & will, yet are they incapable of duty as of
forming any general rule of conduct; their actions
are directed by blind impulse without being capable
of distinguishing right & wrong.   The impulse which
is strongest for the present always prevails & as
that is the constitution of their Nature they cannot
be blamed, they may be noxious, but they cannot be
criminals, they may be objects of like & dislike,
not of approbation and disapprobation.   But with man
it is otherwise.   Indeed, instinct & the blind impulse of our appetites & passions, as in the brute
tribes, influence our actions in our infancy.   By
them we are governed, & not as (?) children and infants, are not considered as capable of obeying Laws
--they are not thought accountable for their actions
--they cannot commit a crime--they are the subjects
of discipline not of blame or disapprobation.   But
when they come to years of Understanding, they act
from principles superior to appetites & passions--
they are capable of considering the consequences of
actions.   They can propose ends to themselves & pros-
ecute them by proper means.   They can reflect on a
course of Life in others & observe the ends they pursue & consider the consequences of these pursuits.
We can choose ends that are best on the whole.   We
blame ourselves when swayed by improper motives, we

are led to do what we will repent of & wish undone;
on the other nothing can give a Virtuous man more
sincere or lasting joy than a consciousness of having
perceived his rectitude unsullied in opposition to
every powerful inducement to abandon it. The consciousness of a wise and worthy conduct will always
inspire with strength of Mind. It encourages the
head of a Man & makes his Countenance to shine; and
the more costly the Sacrifice he has offered at the
shrine of Virtue he will find his triumph the greater.
It appears then from this observation that there is
one kind of actions which we consider as deserving
of applause, another as unworthy. Nor is this distinction grounded on abstract disposition but taken
from the Nature of things. There is a right & a
wrong, something worthy & deserving of approbation,
tho' there were no human being to perceive it. &
other things foolish base & mean. This is the immediate dictate of our natural faculties as well as
the distinction between true & false. If we form an
idea of a man capable of approving perfidy, injustice,
rapine, theft & so on & of disapproving of what was
anyhow good or excellent, we would soon determine
that his Judgement was as erroneous as if he should
think the twice of three equal to fifteen. Now the
Supreme Being infinitely wise & intelligent, discerns human conduct in its finest colours & discovers
whatever in it is worthy or blameable with all its
aggravations & alleviations. His perfect moral character leads him to approve of what is truly worthy
& to disapprove of what is improper. We must therefore conclude that God in his government of rational
creatures, has endowed them with the qualities of
moral & rational agents. Here we may observe that
man is evidently placed here in a state of trial &
probation, where he has access to improve in arts &
knowledge in Virtue and in good Habits. The present
state is intended as a school of disciples & what we
are to expect here is that proper means and induce-
ments be set before us for our improvement, that
proper incitements are held up, to make us avoid
Vice & pursue Virtue, as alone possessing real dig-
nity & alone worthy of our approbation--of this a
little reflection will satisfy us--Here our condition
is such that the good things we enjoy & every evil

118

which we suffer are in some measure within our power.
By this I mean that a man by his foolish conduct may
deprive himself of every enjoyment of life by his
folly & imprudence. He may bring on himself cruel
& tormenting pains that may shorten his days. He
may reduce himself to poverty disgrace and contempt
& make himself the object of public hatred & of public vengeance. In the same manner all our good
things are in some degree in our power as by our
wrong conduct we may deprive ourselves of them--this
then surely is a very strong inducement to look to
our conduct as our enjoyments depend on it. --Fur-
ther--our evils depend much on our conduct--I don't
say all our--For the best men are designed to be
trained to Virtue and happiness by suffering &
trials, but of the common calamities of Life the
greatest part are brought on by ourselves. For if
we trust to those who have made this subject their
study, we will find, that the greatest number of diseases are owing to our intemperance or to some wrong
regimen, good health is generally enjoyed if we use
temperance, proper exercise & a proper regimen. We
see too that Industry is commonly able to furnish
the necessities & the conveniences of life. & if
[by] Providence, they are ever reduced to want & in-
digence, they are entitled to our compassion & will
also always find it, but poverty & all our ills are
generally the consequences of idleness, intemperance
& bad economy. We see also how much our reputation
depends on our conduct. If our conduct is worthy
and irreproachable, whatever our station be will
meet little respect from those who know us. High
ranks may display virtue in brighter colours & with
greater splendor, but in the meanest others will always be amiable and beloved. Thus we see that we
are placed in a state of Discipline, so that our
good enjoyments--even our conduct depend on our conduct. But we may observe further that man is placed
in such a condition, that his conduct also has great
influence on his fellow creatures. So has the divine wisdom seen fit to connect men in Society as he
intended them to live in Society--eventually to assist each other. These circumstances interest us
not only in our own conduct but in that of others;
we are concerned that they should behave properly.

119

Men therefore in such a situation have strong induce-
ments to Virtue, indeed we may observe at the same
time, that the man who seriously intends to pursue
a uniformly upright & worthy behavior will find himself in a state of trial fitted for the exercise &
improvement of his Virtue. And such is our constitution that Virtue is strengthened by exercise as
well as our other habits are. Such then the consequences of good or bad conduct. Great evils follow
sloth, indolence, folly etc. & that tho' not immediately, yet sometimes when the reason which caused it
is forgotten, will it come . . . this is such an administration as might have been expected from the
moral governor of the world. The encouragements of
Virtue & the discouragements of Vice are as strong
as we can suppose in the present state. We are ex-
cited to Virtue by the tendency it has to create power, esteem & all the good and enjoyments of life,
from the inward satisfaction we feel in doing our
duty & the well founded hopes of a future state.
And as to the pains which even the virtuous sometimes are doomed to suffer, this is proper to a
school of discipline & it is by these they are un-
moved in every duty, so that [we?] have reason to
say with the antient servant of God, "It is good for
me that I have been afflicted". And all their sor-
rows here will be abundantly compensated hereafter.
Thus it appears, that in the moral government of the
Supreme Being as well as in his Natural Government,
he acts in a manner suitable to the perfections
which by reason we were enabled to attribute to him.
We may observe at the same time that to form just
notions of the Deity by mere force of our natural
powers requires a greater impartiality and abstract
research than is to be met with in the bulk of men
accustomed only to the objects of Sense, tho' they
may discover in the works of God, evident marks of
his being power & wisdom, yet rude men if left to
trace out his attributes & perfections, will form
conceptions gross & absurd, & far removed from the
account I have now given you.

ENDNOTE for Lect. 86<sup>th</sup>

[15]My experts have been unable to decide just what this Greek word could be.

Hence we find that the doctrines of Natural
Religion have been improved by the Speculations of
Theologians and assisted by the representations of
Deity given in the Sacred Scriptures. For no where
do we find such a completed system of Natural Reli-
gions as in the Christian Writers. The being of
God, is indeed so evident, from his works, & the
conduct of his providence that no nation has been
found so barbarous as to have no notions of Deity,
at all, yet it is to be expected that rude men if
left to trace out his attributes by the mere force
of their reason would form very gross conceptions,
widely different from the presentation of Scripture
& the dictates of a Sound reason. Mr. Hume, in his
Treatise on Natural Religion has endeavored to shew,
that men, especially in the early stages of society,
with regard to their notions of Religion are prone
to idolatry & to the conceiving a plurality of deities
& this no doubt is agreeable to fact as far as we
have access to know, among every nation except the
Jewish. Among all others the grossest notions have
prevailed. Familiarized with objects of sense, they
formed ideas of deities with a human figure and with
human passions. They conceived them as limited in
their Nature & by no means every where present in
the Universe. Each had his different department,
one presided over the Sea, another the Earth--another
the air & so on. They had also deities that belonged
to every family, their Lares, & these everyone worshipped by different rites. They imagined the different heavenly bodies to [have] had different deities & to such extravagance was this spirit of polytheism carried among the Greeks & Romans, that they

had deities to every wood and grove & spring & river --but in all these notions there was nothing rational or that tended to improve the Human Mind. And it is highly probable, that the enlightened writers on Morality among the Greeks & Romans, left out Religion entirely from their system, for this reason, that the notions of Deity publicly established were so absurd and so little suited to promote the practice of Virtue that they could expect no assistance from the principles of Religion, in establishing the Principles of Morality. Of all the 4 Cardinal Virtues Prudence Temperance, Justice & Fortitude, none have any relation to Religion or point out the Deity as an incitement to the practice of them. Nay, in some of these antient systems we find them maintaining that the deities interposed not in the affairs of men, & that however powerfull, yet they had no hand either in the framing or the government of the World. As this is the case those of all that without the aids of Revelation our conceptions of Deity are low, it appears a strange phenomenon, that the Jews who were not more polished & civilized than others, but rather a barbarous people, should have such ideas of deity, his attributes & government as perfectly agreeable to what our reason dictates. They were not Polytheists, they believed in one God the maker of the world, who was eternal omnipotent, omniscient, who had a regard to Virtue & a dislike at Vice. Now such refined notions of Deity in a nation so rude as the Jews, is hardly to be expected unless by a divine Revelation. It is even probable that the notions of polytheism at first arose from a Revelation, but were afterwards corrupted by the heathen nations. Idolatry was introduced and the veneration paid to men of worth and distinguished Virtue was converted into the worship of him as a divinity. Fables formed at first as pieces of moral instruction by degrees gained credit & were received as real stories. The first sentiments of the Deity were thus lost, by the corruptions of human reason, the craft of the priest or the cunning of the politician. We have seen that reason properly employed, will point out the duties of Natural Religion, yet it is necessary to compleat our notions of them, that we be enlightened by a divine revelation.

Having thus laid before you the evidence we have
for the existence & attributes of the Supreme Being
I cannot leave this subject without observing, that
it is of great importance not only to the happiness
of every individual, but to Society in general, to
have just & rational notions of the Deity, his attributes perfections & providence deeply impressed on
the Mind. For,

1. There is no truth within the whole compass
of human knowledge, from which the Mind can derive
such comfort. Is it agreeable to a child to know
that he has a carefull Father whose pleasure is to
rear, educate, support and protect it? The Supreme
Being is the Father of the Universe, the whole world
is his care & has reasonable creatures as his children, so we find him represented in the Sacred writings & by an antient heathen philosopher as quoted
in one of historical Epistles. We are his offspring
and our nature is obedient to his Commands. His wisdom & power were employed in our Creation, & still
are, in our preservation. He pities our weakness
and infirmities as a Father and a Friend, even to
the wicked is he long suffering, patient, and ready
to forgive. His ears are open to the cry of the
young Lions, & much more to the humble and devout
supplications of his rational creatures. In a word,
all his administration is directed by perfect wisdom
& with perfect justice. And tho' we are unable to
comprehend the unbounded scheme of infinite goodness,
yet of this we are sure that neither envy, nor jeal-
ousy, nor any malignant passion can disturb his happiness, or stain his perfections. At present, we
cannot comprehend the plot of this great drama, and
many scenes which shew the skill & intelligence of
the great Poet may appear which we cannot account
for, yet in this we may rest assured that at the
conclusion every difficulty will be resolved & every
incident shine forth as subservient to the design
of the whole. Yet whatever difficulties we may meet
with in this from the weakness of our faculties &
the vast extent of the divine administration, yet a
serious belief of the truths which our reason has
pointed out cannot fail to fill every well disposed
Mind with confidence & joy. The Sun is not more

125

necessary to the beauty & harmony of the Planetary
System than the existence of the Father of the Universe to the comfort of every rational Mind.  Let
the atheist rejoice in the conviction of owing his
being to a fortuitous dance of atoms, & let him rest
in the uncertain hope of a future world to the same
capricious fate.  Surely the atheist has much more
solid ground to rejoice who considers himself as one
of the offspring of God, who loves him & protects
him.  For he who trusts in God need have no other
fear--

"Le erains mon Dieu et je mai d'autre eraint."

2.  A firm belief of the existence of Deity &
of his providence is one of the strongest bonds of
human Society.  By means of his social affections
we see that man was intended for Society & for mutually benefitting each other, but there are some Men
so wicked as to sacrifice all this to their lust of
power or to some favorite passion.  Now the government of God provides some checks to prevent these
from going such lengths as they otherwise would do.
The Contempt of good men--the Civil laws, are strong
restraints upon criminals; but these other crimes of
which the laws have no cognizance--which are above
the law--against these the belief of Deity & dread
of a future Judgement are powerfull guards.  But the
belief of them are not only powerful restraints upon
the worst, but unites the best most firmly in Society.  The Man who considers all as the children of
the same Father, will find every tie of humanity,
justice & benevolence strengthened by the consider-
ations.  And what more powerfull incentive to promote
the good and happiness of our fellow creatures, than
this, that in the same degree we cooperate with the
Almighty & merit his approbation, and that however
our designs may be misconstrued by men, yet they will
not be misrepresented by the great Judge of all the
Earth.  The atheist may complain that religion is the
contrivance of the statesman to strengthen his laws
& give stability to government, by this, he acknowledges that it is one of the strongest bonds of Society which could be contrived.

3. Just & rational sentiments of the Deity are of high importance as they guard us against Superstition. Two causes may be assigned for all the Superstition which has appeared in the world. ① Gross ignorance in the people which has emboldened cunning men to perform tricks among them. The success of this is always in proportion to the ignorance among the people to whom it is first divulged, but it has no connection with religion. ② False notions of Deity, which have led men to believe that he is pleased with penances, & burying themselves in cloisters & sequestrating themselves from active life, such actions however can have no tendency to make men better & the only remedy against them is, the acquiring these notions which reason dictates to us & which Revelation confirms.

Lastly, they have a powerfull influence in promoting & strengthening Virtue--True Religion and Virtue are natural allies & friends & cannot be disjoined without prejudice to both. Without a sense of Religion Virtue would of itself be too weak to restrain the vices of men & Religion without Virtue would be mere hypocrisy or black Superstition. The last has been allowed by all, but that Virtue without Religion is too weak for to restrain the vices of men has been called into question by some, tho', I apprehend on insufficient ground. Lord Shaftesbury seems to be of opinion, that the inculcating the rewards and punishments of another life, as an inducement to Virtue, tends to promote a mercenary disposition, that the real & intrinsic excellence of Virtue is the only inducement that ought to be proposed. In this however his Lordship is not consistent for we find in his Essay on Virtue & Morality that he takes up a contrary opinion, and acknowledges that rational sentiments of the Deity will have a tendency to promote the practice of Virtue in the World. Nor indeed can there be a truth more evident--will not he who believes the existence of Deity & that he delights in Virtue & abhors the workers of iniquity, endeavor to fulfill his pleasure? & render himself agreeable to him by practicing what he approves & avoiding what is displeasing to him? The example of the Supreme Being he sets before him as his pattern

after which to copy, and when the allurements of
Vice are strong the consideration of futurity are
called on to balance them & if on the other hand,
the incitements of Virtue are weak, the prospects
of another world can add sufficient force to them
————  ————  ————-  ————  Since then right notions
of Deity are of such importance both to the individual & to Society, it becomes all of us to think
of them seriously & candidly & endeavor to be established in a firm belief of them. I shall conclude all by recommending to your attention a passage in the works of Cicero De Legibus, Ab. 2. c.
4. when that enlightened philosopher hath expressed
his sentiments on that subject with perspicuity &
elegance ——————————————————————————————— .

Concluded March 3<sup>d</sup>, 1780.

# ABOUT THE AUTHORS

Elmer H. Duncan is Professor of Philosophy at Baylor University. He is the author of a book on Kierkegaard (Waco, Texas: Word Books, 1976) and, some years ago, edited an Index for the First Twenty Volumes of the Journal of Aesthetics and Art Criticism (AMS Press, 1963). He has served as President of the Southwestern Philosophical Society (1974), and currently serves as a Contributing Editor for Leonardo (to which he contributes a column, "Aesthetics for Contemporary Artists," twice yearly). He has published articles in the Journal of the History of Ideas, Ethics, the Journal of Aesthetics and Art Criticism, The Journal of Aesthetic Education, The Southern Journal of Philosophy, The Southwestern Journal of Philosophy, Philosophy and Phenomenological Research, et cetera. He has contributed abstracts to the Bibliography of Philosophy for several years.

He is a Ruling Elder at Central Presbyterian Church, Waco, Texas.

William R. Eakin is a graduate student of philosophy at Baylor University now completing his work for the Master's degree. He received his undergraduate degree from Hendrix College in Arkansas in 1979. His prose and poetry have appeared in various literary magazines and he is currently completing a novel.